Foreword by Dr. Francis Myles

The
Revelation
Of
JESUS CHRIST

...Rediscovering the Gospel of Christ!

By

Apostle Lee Roberson

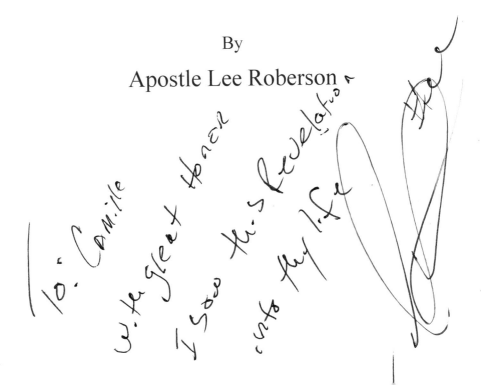

To: Camille
W. te great honor
I seeo this Revelatio
into my life

Published by:
Sons of God Embassy
Kingsland, Georgia

For Worldwide Distribution

Printed in the United States

Cover Design by: WORKINPERKINS

Edited by: Karen Hosey

Publisher is not responsible for websites (or their content)
if not owned by the publisher

Acknowledgments

THE GREATEST COMPLIMENT we can give the Father is when we "become" what He designed us to be. On the journey of "becoming" we have help from friends and foes, family and strangers, and blessings and cursings because all of our experiences and relationships have a role to play on our quest to "become" God's creation. I want to acknowledge the impact that the following men and women of God have had on my life during my journey. Special acknowledgment and thanks goes to:

- Urana Moore for all the help in editing of this book. Your help is greatly appreciated.

- My mom and dad, Gloria and Bobby Roberson. Thank you for raising me in the nurture and admonition of the Lord. The example you set and the godly life you lived still guides my life even to this day.

- My spiritual mother, Carmela Real Myles who has been a great anchor and support of my ministry. I thank God for such a woman.

- My spiritual father Apostle Francis Myles. He has been a true father in every sense of the word. His teaching, The Order of Melchezidek, is solely responsible for this revelation that I have been trusted to give to the Body of Christ.

- My church family, Sons of God Embassy, you are such a jewel to pastor and lead. The love and honor that you have given me over the years, have been priceless seeds that have led to our first harvest, this book, The Divine Revelation of Jesus Christ. Bless you all, Pops

- A special thank you to Karen Hosey who has been such an incredible wealth of insight and guidance that has truly blessed me. Your insight is truly priceless! Thank you, woman, of God.

- The greatest wife a man can ask for, April Roberson. God has been so kind to me to entrust me with such a woman as April Roberson. Through every pain, set back, and mistake she has been there. My greatest encourager and supporter, thank you seems so little for the sacrifices you have made for me. I love you and thank God for you and your life I am truly a blessed man to have such jewel in my life.

Endorsements

THE BRAIN SUPERVISES all human activities. This includes everything from the involuntary beat of the heart to the conscious decisions that are made. It controls hearing, sight, smell, speech, appetite, learning and every aspect of human behavior. Individual traits, temperament, physical growth, and all the other characteristics inherited at birth are controlled by the brain. The mind or the intellect is a major part of the brain. It is also influenced by inherited temperament. The mind is the principal place of memory. This is where we make deductions, judgments, and decisions. It has been said that it is the mind that makes the body rich. This is true because it is through the mind that we become aware of God, His Word, and His plan of salvation through Jesus Christ. The mind is where the battle rages for the human soul.

This is why Satan tries so hard to control the human intellect and why the Holy Spirit is ever wooing and encouraging us. Peter said in (2 Peter 3:1) to stir up their pure minds (v. 1). Their minds were pure. They were single-minded Christians. Their commitment to Christ was genuine. Nevertheless, it was appropriate to stir them up. We all need to be aroused from time to time. If not, we may live in the same way day after day. Our daily lives may become too routine. There is always the danger of becoming lukewarm, formal, and acting from habit rather than from a conscious desire to please God.

Apostle Lee did a wonderful job with this book; the book brings us face to face with fresh views of old verses that will open the eyes of many to their real meanings. With candor and humor, he makes the scriptures speak to our times and our problems, and that is the business of a Christian expositor above all else, good job son."

~ Dr. Bobby Roberson, Pastor
Bethlehem Christian Fellowship Ministry, Inc

I met the author some years ago, when he was first entering into ministry. He questioned me concerning going into ministry and my advice to him was to sincerely pray and I gave him the keys to my office. From that time until this day he embarked on an early morning and noonday and late night journey with God through prayer. He covenanted to talk with God and God in turn talks with him as evidenced by the revelation he has received of Jesus Christ in this book.

Unfortunately, in many of today's churches, Jesus Christ has become a side note. Ask the average Christian, "Who is Jesus?" and they will not be able to correctly answer ("Always be prepared to give an answer to everyone who asks you to give the reason for the hope that you have." 1 Peter 3:15). In this book, Apostle Roberson unlocks the mysteries of the revelation of Jesus Christ. He efficaciously seats Christ back to His proper place in the church and the heart of man.

Some will read this work, agree with some of its teachings and principles, but be unwilling to accept its call and ideologies. Others, that agree on the instinctive level, will be intimidated by the traditional standards and find many of the book's positions challenged by these norms, and will reject the truth in this book. There are still others that will read this book, agree with it, and put its principles into practice and I guarantee this action will transfigure your spiritual walk, growth, and life!

~ *Larry W. Curry, Th. D., Pastor.*

The Revelation of Jesus Christ

Foreword

I AM VERY PROUD of the work, my spiritual son, Apostle Lee Roberson has done in writing this life-changing book, <u>The Revelation of Jesus Christ</u>. As the title of the book suggests, there is no higher revelation on both sides of heaven that the children of the Kingdom can aspire to than the revelation of Jesus Christ.

Without question, this is the great mystery of our faith: Christ was revealed in a human body and vindicated by the Spirit. He was seen by angels and announced to the nations. He was believed in throughout the world and taken to heaven in glory (1 Timothy 3:16).

One of the most important mysteries of God is the mystery of the incarnation. Saint Paul tells us that the incarnation of Christ (God) into the human body is a "great mystery." Unfortunately, many ecclesiastical leaders and believers do not understand this great mystery. Many believers do not understand why the Word became flesh. After the fall of Adam and Eve in the Garden of Eden, humankind became shrouded completely in sin. The fall of Adam and Eve was so drastic that sin invaded every fiber of man's triune being. Man's spirit lost the life of God, his soul also became a prisoner of sin while death attached itself to man's body. Sin in the human nature spread like a malignant cancer to every fiber of man's being.

A total overhaul of man's entire nature was required. Humankind needed a brand-new spirit, soul, and body. What's more, sin had destroyed humankind's God-given capacity to become like God and represent Him fully. When Christ (the eternal Word and Image of God) saw the utter depravity of humankind's condition, He knew that the only way humankind could ever become like God was if He became one of us. Thus, the Word became flesh through the virgin birth and God became one of us.

- For a child is born to us, a son is given to us. The government will rest on his shoulders. And he will be called: Wonderful Counselor, Mighty God, Everlasting Father, Prince of Peace (Isaiah 9:6).

- Therefore, from now on, we regard no one according to the flesh. Even though we have known Christ according to the flesh, yet now we know Him thus no longer. Therefore, if anyone is in Christ, he is a new creation; old things have passed away; behold, all things have become new (2 Corinthians 5:16-17 NKJV).

These Scriptures are probably two of the most misunderstood passages in the Bible. We can never appreciate who Christ and Jesus really are if we remain ignorant as to what really transpired in both the incarnation and the resurrection. In Isaiah 9:6, the prophet Isaiah makes two very important prophetic statements that we need to understand if we want to know Christ the hope of glory. The prophet tells us that "a Child was born to us" and that "a Son was given to us." Herein lies the entire mystery of Christ's incarnation. The Child who was born is Jesus of Nazareth. The Son who was given to us is Christ (the eternal Word and Image of God) (See John 1:1.) In The Revelation of Jesus Christ, Apostle Lee Roberson does a masterful job of deepening our understanding of the Gospel of Christ. This book is truly one of the best books ever written on the important subject of "Christology!" I highly recommend it to Christ seekers all over the world.

~ *Dr. Francis Myles*

Bestselling Author: The Order of Melchizedek

Senior Pastor: Royal Priesthood International Embassy, Tempe, AZ

The Revelation of Jesus Christ

Preface

IN FEBRUARY 2015, my life changed forever. I was given an opportunity to teach in my spiritual father's school of ministry in the country of Zimbabwe. The topic was, The Order of Melchizedek and the Manifest Sons of God.

Little did I know I was being chosen for this special revelation that you are now accessing. In this book, you will discover that there is a graduation coming to the Body of Christ. "What kind of graduation?" you ask. It's a graduation from your humanity to your deity. The mystery of Christ is about to be known and revealed to you. In this book, you will see how Adam and Eve were stripped of their deity, by receiving a gospel that is still active today. This book will reveal to you the state and health of the church worldwide. So I say to you, your spiritual hunger is about to be increased as you receive the truths that this book brings to you. Your spiritual hunger will not be wasted. You will be filled!!!

Yours truly,
Apostle Lee Roberson
Senior Pastor, Sons of God Embassy, Kingsland, Georgia

Table of Contents

1

WHY IS THE CHURCH STUCK?

I WANT TO SHARE with you why I believe the church body is stuck. Ephesians 4:13 says, *"Till we all come to the unity of the faith and of the knowledge of the Son of God, to a perfect man, to the measure of the stature of the fullness of Christ"* (NKJV). There is a dimension of Kingdom living that the Church has not yet stepped into. I believe there is a reason we are not walking in the truth of that scripture yet. Let me explain.

There are three numbers I want to introduce to you in this chapter that will give a very strong prophetic insight into the state of the church today. The numbers are 12, 18, and 30. Now, to make this simple, God is a spirit; He is not flesh and blood. If He has a son His son must be Spirit also. We know that a spirit cannot give birth to flesh: a spirit can only give birth to spirit! This is why when Nicodemus came to Jesus in John 6:6, Jesus said, *"That which is born of the flesh is flesh, and that which is born of the Spirit is spirit."* He was trying to show him how he could access the "Christ nature!" Unfortunately, the church has turned this powerful scripture into a reference for water baptism, missing its entire meaning.

Isaiah 9:6a (NKJV) states, *"For unto us a Child is born, Unto us a Son is given."* Jesus represents God's humanity; Christ represents God's Deity. Mary could give birth to God's humanity, i.e., Jesus, but she could not give birth to his Deity, i.e., Christ. Christ had to be given. Jesus was born to deal with our humanity so we could have access to a clean and perfect bloodline: therefore, we now have a righteous DNA. Jesus had to bleed on the cross, so our sins would be washed away; however, Christ, who is the Spirit of God, does not bleed, because He (God's deity) is an eternal Spirit. By the way, it is important for us to understand that "Christ," is not Jesus' last name! The Lord Jesus has no last name! This is because your last name does not speak to your assignment but speaks of your natural lineage. Adam was not given a last name when he was created: he was just Adam. Last names connect you to earthly power and human lineage.

"Till we all come to the unity of the faith and of the knowledge of the Son of God, to a perfect man, to the measure of the stature of the fullness of Christ" (NKJV). Ephesians 4:13

Notice that when the Holy Spirit inspired Apostle Paul to write this, he did not say we are to come to the fullness of Jesus (humanity) but of Christ (deity). In other words, it is in Christ, the deity of God, that we will come to the full measure of the stature of the fullness of the Son of God! There was a movie in 2011 entitled "Limitless." The idea behind this movie was a pill, that when taken, would give a person access to 100% of his brain, granting him limitless power and limitless knowledge. According to the movie we use only 10% of our brain. While this statement has not been proven,

I think it is evident that we lost some use of our brain power after the fall of man. After all, Adam had the mental capacity to name all of the insects (there are over 12 million), plants (there are over one million), and animals (there are over 1.5 million) species, yet we have difficulty today remember passwords! One can easily say we're not using the same capacity of our brain as Adam. However, if we enter into the fullness of Christ (deity) I believe what we lost in the fall will be restored to us. So as in the movie, Christ (the deity of God) is like the pill, returning the limitless ability we lost in the fall. Jesus was 100% man and 100% God: He was the perfect harmony between deity and humanity. This is the blessing of the revelation of Jesus Christ to those that are hungry enough to pursue this revelation.

There are three numbers that directly deals with Jesus and will provide insight into why the Body of Christ is stuck. Each of these numbers have a prophetic meaning so they will give us insight into what our Lord is trying to show us pertaining to the Body of Christ. The numbers are: 12, 18, and 30. The Biblical meaning of these numbers are as follows:

12 – Government and Power
18 – Bondage and Suffering
30 – Authority and Maturity

Jesus was 100% man and 100% God: He was the perfect harmony between deity and humanity.

These three numbers are connected to the Lord Jesus Christ but I will show how each of these numbers affects the Body of Christ. Let's take the number 12 and see how it affects Jesus and the Body of Christ today.

> *"and when He was twelve years old, they went up to Jerusalem according to the custom of the feast. When they had finished the days, as they returned, the Boy Jesus lingered behind in Jerusalem. And Joseph and His mother did not know it; but supposing Him to have been in the company, they went a day's journey, and sought Him among their relatives and acquaintances. So when they did not find Him, they returned to Jerusalem, seeking Him. Now so it was that after three days they found Him in the temple, sitting in the midst of the teachers, both listening to them and asking them questions. And all who heard Him were astonished at His understanding and answers. So when they saw Him, they were amazed; and His mother said to Him, "Son, why have you done this to us? Look, your father and I have sought you anxiously." And He said to them, "Why did you seek me? Did you not know that I must be about My Father's business?" But they did not understand the statement, which He spoke to them. Then He went down with them and came to Nazareth, and was subject to them, but His mother kept all these things in her heart. And Jesus increased in wisdom and stature, and in favor with God and men.* Luke 2: 42-52 (NKJV)

We see Jesus, at a young tender age of 12, in the temple where all who heard him were astonished at his understanding and answers: they were amazed because of the wisdom that he demonstrated for one so young. The scripture is silent on how Jesus came to be in the temple but is clear that Joseph and Mary thought he was with the caravan going home. It is safe to assume that He had been in the temple earlier and did not hear the call that it was time to leave. As a result, his parents were not aware that he was not with the group. When they discovered he was not, they frantically returned to the city to find Him. Jesus was missing for three days. His mother and father would represent your spiritual mother and father of today. Jesus, despite having great wisdom, did not have the blessing from his mother and father and had not been properly released from them to minister. How many times have we, in our zeal and excitement, gone off to do things for the Lord without seeking the guidance and blessing of our spiritual covering?

The next point I want to bring is powerful, Jesus' mother and father confronted Him in the temple. *"So when they saw Him, they were amazed; and His mother said to Him, "Son, why have you done this to us? Look, your father and I have sought you anxiously"* (verse 48). Though He was amazed that they didn't realize He had to be about His "Father's business" we see in verse 51 that he went down with them and subjected Himself to them. God showed me that many men and women will begin to return to their spiritual mother and father, realizing they can't go further until they submit to their authority. At the beginning, I taught that 12 means governmental power and even though Jesus is sent to change, bless and transform the world, at age12 he is not ready. He has wisdom, he has power, but He still missing something; he is missing the authority to act. Thus, He must submit to his mother and father and return home with them.

Many confuse "power" and "authority": power is the capacity or ability to act while authority is the right to exercise power. Power is something one can receive through studying the Word of God, praying and fasting; e.g., you acquire the ability to activate the Word of God in your life and become a minister of the gospel. However, that power or ability alone does not confer on you the authority, i.e., the right, to perform marriages. You must be given the authority or right to exercise that power in performing a marriage ceremony as a minister of the gospel. At the age of 12 Jesus has the power (ability) but he was still subject to the authority of his parents.

It was necessary for Jesus to submit to his mother and father; even the Savior needed more growth before He could fulfill His true assignment. His obedience killed a seed or the potential of that seed to overtake him, and that seed is called the bastard seed. (This will be explained in a later chapter of this book entitled "Destroying the Bastard Seed.") At age 12 he was not ready to be offered up as our perfect sacrifice. If Jesus had to submit to authority and take the time to develop and prepare for his assignment, how much more should you and I submit properly to our spiritual mother and father until we are ready to walk in our assignment?

The next number we will look at is 18 which connects to bondage or suffering. We must understand this if we are to understand the Bible when it says "if we suffer with Him we will also reign with Him."

We have taken the concept of suffering with Christ and made it into all kinds of things that are not accurate. The concept of suffering with Christ in Scripture has to do with going against the will of man to bring the will of God into existence. Over the next decade many of us will have to go against the will of men in a fallen world that believes that a man can marry another man and a woman can marry another woman. The Bible teaches us to obey the laws of the land but when the laws of the land do not line up with the law of God, we don't have to obey them. This is another type of suffering. The children of Israel were oppressed for 18 years. Luke 13:11 tells us of the woman who had an infirmity for 18 years. Judges 10:8 speaks of the Ammonites who oppressed the Israelites for 18 years. As you can see 18 is connected to bondage or a type of suffering. Remember the Bible says in Hebrews 5:8 that Jesus learned obedience through the things He suffered. Suffering is used by the Spirit of God to develop character and humility. Jesus, the Savior of the world, Who, in fact, came to save Mary and Joseph, must submit Himself to them. He had to return home and subject himself to them in obedience. That is a perfect example of suffering, to submit to a person of lower authority. The greatest objective of our suffering is to teach us obedience; and if Jesus had to learn it, is it possible that He didn't already possess it? If He had to learn obedience through suffering, who are we to think we can escape it? This is why we see so many undeveloped people in the church today: they do not want to suffer so that they may be fully developed: they want to skip this step and go straight to greatness. Suffering prepares us that we may finish our course. Every son must suffer to become. This is what is holding back many in the church today, the desire for quick results, quick answers, quick ordinations and quick promotion. It is through our willingness to spend time in preparation that God separates sons from bastards.

A son will suffer that he may be developed to fulfill his assignment in the earth.

The next number we will look at is 30. Luke 3:22-23 says, *"And the Holy Ghost descended in a bodily shape like a dove upon him, and a voice came from heaven, which said, Thou art my beloved Son; in thee I am well pleased. And Jesus himself began to be about thirty years of age, being (as was supposed) the son of Joseph, which was the son of Heli."* We see Jesus at age 30 and he has just come to John to be baptized. Thirty is the number that deals with maturity:

- Joseph was 30 when he became 2nd in command to Pharaoh.
- The priest officially entered service at age 30.
- David became king when he was 30.
- Ezekiel was called by God as a prophet at age 30.
- John the Baptist was 30 when he came out of the wilderness and paved the way for Jesus himself.

Jesus, after 18 years of preparation through the suffering of obedience, is now ready to receive his authority. At age 30 he hears these words *"This is my beloved son in whom I am well pleased."* The Father can now transfer to the Son what he couldn't give him at 12 in the temple prior to the 18 years of preparation. He receives something at 30 that signifies Sonship and announces to the world that He is now ready to fulfil His assignment. He is now mature. Many in the Body of Christ have wisdom, many have power, but they don't have authority and character because they've not endured the suffering that is required to develop them in those areas. A perfect example is how a butterfly develops. When the caterpillar creates the cocoon, it begins the process of metamorphosis which changes him from a crawling caterpillar to a soaring butterfly but his development is incomplete until he emerges from the cocoon. The process of getting out of the cocoon produces pressure on his fragile wings. It is a slow and painful process, however, if he doesn't go through that process himself, if someone chips at the cocoon to "help", the butterfly will emerge but will never be able to fly. It is the pressure (suffering) applied to his wings that enables him to have the strength he needs to soar and fulfill his purpose. What we are about to witness is many in the church being prepared and developed through suffering to enable them to fulfill their assignment. This process will give the Father true sons and daughters that have suffered for His namesake. Jesus is a seed that will produce a harvest of sons. Let's look at Romans 8:29 *"For whom he did foreknow, he also did predestinate to be conformed to the image of his Son, that he might be the firstborn among many brethren."* In this passage, Paul teaches us that there are more sons yet to be manifested. The reason the church has been stuck is because many in the church have skipped the process of preparation: in their youth (the beginning of their journey) they failed to submit to their spiritual covering. When the Body of Christ allows preparation and maturity to run its course you will see the greatest power, the greatest authority, the greatest character, and the greatest nature of God's being witnessed on planet earth. As you take this journey in reading this book I pray you see each number as a step and examine yourself and see where you may have aborted the process of becoming.

"Pray this with me: *Heavenly Father, I gladly come before you with an open heart, and I am ready to give myself fully to you and the Kingdom of God. I acknowledge that I have skipped one of these steps and I give your Spirit permission to guide me back to the step that I need to complete that I may be offered up as my elder brother was offered up as perfect sacrifice Thank you, in Jesus' name, Amen."*

2

THE MIND OF CHRIST

For "who has known the mind of the Lord that he may instruct Him? "But we have the mind of Christ. 1 Corinthians 2:16

IN THIS chapter, I want you to understand this very important fact: the mind is a very powerful instrument, an instrument for change or for destruction. Based upon the input received, the mind can be directed toward the heights of heaven or the sorrows of earth. When you understand this fact you will begin to walk in a new awareness. You will be able to move in the spirit in ways you never imagined. With that said, let's begin.

Whenever God wants to do something in our lives, He sends Christ. Whenever He wants something accomplished, He sends Christ. Whenever He wants victory, He sends Christ. Remember, Christ is the deity of God. In order to walk and fully maintain this teaching (and the revelation of it), the first thing we will need to do is change our mindset. There's no question the condition of our mind must be altered. There are a few things I want to say about the mind before going deeper into this lesson.

Firstly, the healthiness of your mind is determined by what your mind constantly sees or what your mind is continually exposed to. The reason a lot of us are not successful is because of what our minds are continuously absorbing. The reason we're not moving in the power or the spirit of Christ, is due to where and on what we are continually focusing our attention, i.e., our mind. Just imagine what would happen in your life if you were to listen to the Word of God continuously? How healthy would your mind be? Because your mind feeds your body, how healthy would your body be if your mind fed on the Word of God continually?

THE MOUNTAIN OF TRANSFIGURATION

"Now after six days Jesus took Peter, James, and John, and led them up on a high mountain apart by themselves; and He was transfigured before them. His clothes became shining, exceedingly white, like snow, such as no launderer on earth can whiten them." Mark 9:2-3

On the mountain of transfiguration, Jesus was transformed in the presence of three of His disciples, Peter, James and John. In Mark 9:2-3 the scripture teaches us that Jesus' garment became as white as snow. However, his head didn't change. Jesus is the head of the body. The head represents the mind. His garment represented the body, which also represents Christ's body of believers. As we focus our mind on the things of God we bring into manifestation the scripture that says we "have the mind of Christ" (1 Corinthians 2:16). As our minds become healthy, as we are cleansed and made pure by the work of the Holy Spirit, our bodies will also become healthy; we too will be transformed. We will no longer be sick, contaminated, and unable to receive from our head or from our Christ-mind. This scripture is giving us insight into what is about to happen to us. We're getting ready to have an epiphany! I want you to get really excited! We are getting ready to enter a spiritual awakening. We are about to receive what's in God's mind!

> *For the weapons of our warfare are not carnal but mighty in God for pulling down strongholds, casting down arguments and every high thing that exalts itself against the knowledge of God, bringing every thought into captivity to the obedience of Christ, 2 Corinthians 10:4-5 (NKJV)*

Before we go any further let me share an experience I had with Christ. God blessed me with this revelation in 2015 and I began 2016 with a pursuit and hunger that I have never had before. I went on a 21day water fast. From the book of Acts to the book of Revelation there are over 500 scriptures that mention Jesus Christ or Christ Jesus. I took all 500 scriptures and I put myself on a very tight prayer schedule to pray and quote them every 21hrs. I determined to pray at least 21 of the scriptures three times a day. Then I downloaded all 500 scriptures on my phone. For 21 days, I would walk twice a day listening to the scriptures. It took an hour and a half for me to listen to them all. I did this for 21days. Then it happened! It was June 12th approximately 3:30 am I was up praying and I was taken in a vision with "CHRIST" (not Jesus). I quickly noticed that I was inside my mind; yes, you read right, I was inside my mind. I saw my thoughts running freely in mind. Shortly thereafter, to my right, I saw this glorious and huge figure that had the shape of a man all the while

I felt majestic, beauty and love, all at the same time. As he stood next to me I saw a thought in my mind begin to take shape. Christ shooed away my thought the way you would shoo away a fly. My thought fell and did not continue taking shape but shortly after the thought fell I saw an image being formed. As the image got bigger and began to take shape I saw Christ rise in front of the image. He spoke one word with great authority, He shouted "NO" and the image was shattered when he shouted. I felt everything in my mind shift. He began to speak to me and said the thought is the décor to occupy you until the image is established in your mind. Then I noticed we were no longer in my mind; we were suddenly in His mind. I immediately felt peace like I never felt or had explained to me before! He was so beautiful and elegant. He was this glorious white that can't be found on earth; His mind was so clear and beautiful you could see as far your eyes would allow you. But suddenly I felt the spirit of loneliness and I remember saying within myself "Why am I feeling loneliness?" He answered me swiftly. He said "What you are feeling is not loneliness as you know it but rather you are feeling absence." I said "Absence?" He said, "Yes. You and the Body of Christ are not occupying my mind so you are "absent", that's why you feel loneliness." He then led me to 2 Corinthians 10:5, *"Casting down arguments and every high thing that exalts itself against the Knowledge of God, bringing every thought into captivity to the obedience of CHRIST."* Then I saw it, what I had overlooked all these year; we must surrender our thoughts to <u>Christ</u>, the <u>deity</u> of God. He went on to explain that I can't cast down what I did not plant; He said, "I am the one that gives power to that scripture. You must submit to Me and let Me cast it down the way you witnessed me do in your mind. I want to do that for all of My people."

Let's go to 2 Corinthians 10:4. It says, *"For the weapons of our warfare are not carnal, but mighty in God for the pulling down of strong holds. Casting down imaginations (arguments)."* Let's replace the term "imagination" with the word "arguments." We're doing this simply because in most cases your carnal mind is arguing with God. Your carnal mind is constantly arguing with the deity of God. Your carnal mind is also constantly arguing with the power of God being in your life. The arguments in your mind are stopping God from manifesting His glory in your life. Verse 5 says, "Casting down arguments and every high thing that exalted itself against the knowledge of God, and bringing into captivity every thought into the obedience of Christ." In essence, the Bible is saying if you're going to have a healthy mind, your carnal thoughts need to be cast down or destroyed by Christ. In other words, your thoughts need to be put under arrest! Our carnal thoughts are the reason we find ourselves in so much trouble.

The mind can be directed toward the heights of
heaven or the sorrows of earth.

HOLDING YOUR THOUGHTS CAPTIVE!

Let us examine the second portion of the verse above "the knowledge of God" The depth of your knowledge of God determines if you will argue with God or trust Him. If you don't know much about God and your knowledge of Him and His word is limited, then whenever He speaks to you about something He's trying to do in your life, it will be difficult for you to comprehend because you are not on that level of understanding yet. For example, a lot of people will argue about God's ability to heal because of their lack of knowledge in that area. Another example would be in the most well-known area of sowing and reaping. How many Christians struggle with practicing what God's Word says about giving and receiving? Because they lack understanding of this principle they don't trust God or have faith in what He said. Thus, when they have a need and the Spirit of God tells them to give they hesitate or refuse because they fear not having enough rather than trusting in God's Word. The sad thing is when God tells them to sow He is trying to move on their behalf to fill a need for their benefit. Because their knowledge of God is limited they will start arguing with God, instead of simply obeying Him.

It is my prayer that you are going to change this inaccurate pattern of behavior because you're getting ready to walk in the fullness of Christ. You're getting ready to be centered in Him. I am convinced that there will be a generation of Kingdom citizens who will walk in the full manifestation of the revelation of Christ, before His second coming. The church has been arguing with God for too long. He has been trying to tell us for decades to come to the place of true Sonship. The Spirit of God wants to bring us into the full measure of the full stature of Christ (Ephesians 4:12)! As we strive to move closer to Him, we must identify areas of our lives that are against His word and stop arguing with the Holy Spirit.

THE POWER TO FINISH

One of the many blessings of the spirit of Christ is the ability to finish. The knowledge of Christ should make many of us very happy. I remember a time when I became real slothful with my prayer life. Let me share this experience with you. I was in a time of prayer, in fact, I was in a time of nonstop prayer and worship. I was in pursuit of something from the Lord and though I had been praying all day, I had not yet received the answer that I was seeking. I sat on the couch to watch television and drifted off to sleep. Because I had sown several hours of prayer and worship the Spirit realm was fertile and pregnant but because I did not press in until I received the answer, even though the atmosphere was pregnant with my prayers and worship, the enemy used the frequency of the television to steal my answer. This is why we must learn to press until Christ is finished and we receive what we are seeking. Romans 8:26 says, *"Likewise the Spirit (Christ) also helps in our weakness. For we do not know what we should pray for as we ought, but the Spirit Himself makes intercession for us with groaning which cannot be uttered."* He is waiting to finish what we start.

When Christ takes over your mind He's going to cause you to finish and finish well. When we have the mind of Christ we will get tired of almost finishing or just coming "close." We need to finish and finish strong! When the mind of Christ comes upon you and it takes root in you He will take root in you. You will take on a different dimension of living. Things that you used to abort, things that you used to turn away from and lose focus on, you will find yourself finishing. Where there are areas of your life where you easily got weary Christ will infuse you with supernatural strength to go the distance and finish the course.

One of the many blessings of the spirit of
Christ is the ability to finish.

However, for all of this to be possible in this season of our lives we must learn to ask for divine help. Many of us must move away from our prideful stubbornness and ask Him to intervene. This brings Moses to mind. When he sent twelve spies to spy out the promise land, they gathered huge grapes to show how rich the land was. The Bible is clear; one man could not carry all the grapes by himself. Each man in the camp of spies needed the help of the others to carry the bountiful produce of the land. Each man still got their blessing, but they needed each other's help. Needing the help of others does not mean you're not strong. It just proves that you have humility. Many people think that doing it by themselves makes them strong; it actually shows our unbroken selfishness. If Jesus needed the help of His twelve disciples, and He is the savior of the world, how can we believe we are equipped to excel on our own? Praise God, we don't have to!

THE SPIRIT OF THE MIND

I'm so excited that in Ephesians 4:23 the Bible says, "Be renewed in the spirit of your mind." Do you know what the word "renewed" means? It means to be "renovated." I'm sure the first thing entering your mind is its relationship to a home. The word "renovate" also means "repetitiously" or on a repeated basis. In essence, God is saying He's getting ready to give you a renovation. This renovation must be done on a repeated basis; it is not a one-time effort, it requires repetitive action. Please remember when a choice is made to renovate a house there is usually nothing wrong with the house, it just needs to be upgraded. God wants to renovate the house of your mind. He won't redo the whole house; He will just alter the material inside the house that is stopping it from reaching its full beauty. Glory to God! Get excited because your mind is being upgraded to the mind of Christ! He's not giving you a new mind since your mind has already received the seed of Christ. The Lord is renovating your mind, because there are some things in your mind that must be removed for you to step into the full inheritance of what He has for you.

Many of God's people have planted negative things in their minds such as failures, pain, and old grievances. These weeds in the mind must be removed! When a renovation is done the structure or shell is already there; it is the gutting of the inside of the structure that takes place. Before the renovations begin, construction specialists are brought in to provide advice, counsel and guidance based on what you are trying to accomplish. In the natural, many of us like to collect things. These things may take up quite a bit of space in our homes. What God wants us to understand is that our memories do the same thing to our minds. Whenever we try to collect something new, the old things get in the way leaving no room for the new. Have you seen the TV program, "The Hoarders"? It's about people who are unable to let go of anything; they collect things until sometimes it reaches the ceiling of their home. A specialist is needed to come in and help them get rid of the clutter; he or she helps them do what they could not do themselves. God is that specialist! God is about to clear out the clutter and expand the capacity of your mind so He can step in and occupy your thoughts. God will help you "hold your mind under the captivity of Christ" so you can walk in "the deity of God."

I am going to assume that most of you are like me and you hold on to things. You may hold onto clothing, jewelry, notes, or even copies of old contacts (mothers often save their kids school papers, drawings, and such). What we must understand is that everything we hold on to is connected to a person, place or thing. Unfortunately, everything we hold onto gets a portion of our soul. Take people for instance, whether a person was good to you or not, they still get a portion of you when they exit your life. Most of us are still carrying people who are no longer in our lives because we're still holding onto old memories. Unfortunately, when we try to move in the deity of God we struggle, because "these old memories" are still connected to us and hinder our ability to receive new instruction and experiences from God.

Anyone who has walked with God knows that He doesn't talk a lot. They also know that when He does speak, even two or three words will change your life forever. Just think about that for a minute. You could be around someone who has been talking to you for hours, and your life is still the same. However, when God speaks, three words can alter your entire existence because every word is connected to life. Jesus said, "The words I speak are spirit and life." To paraphrase, God is saying to us, "I'm giving you two things: I'm giving you my spirit and I'm giving you my life." This is why when God speaks He doesn't have to say a paragraph; He can just release two words and it will erase everything that has been done in your life if received in faith. This can occur as we listen to God's Word read or spoken to us. *"But he who is spiritual judges all things, yet He Himself is rightly judged by no one. For who has known the mind of the Lord that he may instruct him? But we have the mind of Christ."*

Every word that is spoken is collected,
stored and compartmentalized until there is
no room in the mind.

1 Corinthians 2:15-16

We received the mind of Christ when we became born again, we just need a spiritual renovation. Every word that is spoken to us becomes a fixture in our mind if we don't immediately decide to save or discard it. For example, if you were told "you're not going to amount to anything! No one in your family has ever accomplished that!" and you accepted that thought, it resides in your subconscious and can impact your decisions and behaviors for many years. Parents often don't realize the damage that is done to their children when they say things like that to them as they make childish mistakes. Every word that is spoken is collected, stored and compartmentalized until there is no room for the mind of Christ. God sends a specialist (the Holy Spirit) to come in your mind to conduct some deep housecleaning, and if the mess is great enough, an actual renovation is required.

ISSUES

Earlier on we discussed the things that affect our mind, we said the mind absorbs what it is constantly exposed to or sees. There are three areas of interest:

a) Family issues

b) Financial issues

c) Identity issues - inner turmoil

Firstly, let's look closely at family issues. A wife may be distracted with things taking place in her home instead of focusing on the promise that her whole household will be saved. The problem is that God didn't specify a date it was going to take place; He just indicated that it would take place. The woman who is believing God for her husband's salvation must understand that there is a season for everything. Her time for salvation came up first. Instead of being focused and distracted on her husband's salvation she should be focused on her own spiritual growth and development. She must accept the fact that her husband hasn't made up his mind to surrender to God yet. Her job is to continually pray and intercede for her husband but unfortunately other people, our own desire, and sometimes even the enemy, will put us under pressure that we must **do** something. We then apply pressure on everyone else. It is the Holy Spirit's job to bring them to a place of conviction and repentance; it is our job to pray for them and love them so that they will be drawn to the love of God – for it is the *"Love of God that draws men to repentance"* (Romans 2:4). Sometimes our minds become pre-occupied with things that have not been put in our hands to carry out, things we cannot bring to pass with our own effort. We must remember that not even Jesus knows the exact date for the end of this age. According to Scripture, that is in the Father's hand. When our mind is focused on the wrong things, we can't move in the deity of God. God wants us to give Him our undivided attention.

Do you honestly believe that Jesus was caught off guard when Judas Iscariot committed suicide? Do you think He walked with this man and didn't know he was going to commit suicide? I don't think so! Remember, this same Jesus told Nathaniel, "Before Phillip called you I saw you under the fig tree." Having the mind of Christ enables us to know and discern things that are beyond the capability of our carnal mind. Imagine walking with someone while knowing that the sentence of death is upon him or her and not be affected negatively by it? Jesus knew what was in store for Him, but still went ahead and gave His life on the cross. He was not moved negatively by any of it. This was because He had the mind of Christ. When you have the mind of Christ, you respond the way God would respond in any situation. Can you see the importance and value of putting on the "mind of Christ"?

Jesus was betrayed and abandoned by His disciples at the most critical time in His earthly ministry. The Bible shows us that He was teaching His faithful followers every day for at least three years. He was also feeding those same disciples and their families for three and half years. He showered them with love for three and half years. However, in the hardest moment of His life, He looked around and all of them had fled: every one of them ran away and rejected Him. Yet, He had the ability to overcome such deep rejection. In the midst of it all, He had the presence of mind to stand up and declare, "I am never alone. My father is always with me." That is the mind of Christ! When we don't have this "mind" in us, God has to send a special messenger to help us put on the mind of Christ. We are too often fixated on all the meaningless activity and conversation taking place around us. What we don't understand is that we may actually be hindering someone's deliverance because we're failing to plug into the mind of Christ. We're stopping someone's breakthrough because we feel the pressing need to change someone's opinion through an argumentative spirit. Many of us are becoming counterproductive to the work of God, because we're not trusting God to change people around us His way. We must abide in the mind of Christ. Do you remember when Peter denied Jesus three times? Do you think Jesus didn't know that Peter was going deny Him? He knew that Peter would and yet His mind stayed focused on offering Himself on the cross as our sin bearer. He never allowed His mind to be preoccupied with what Peter, Judas and the rest of His disciples were doing. Had He allowed His mind to be swayed by these distractions He would have never fulfilled His Kingdom assignment. We must remain steadfast and not fall prey to unnecessary distractions. When we put on the mind of Christ, we have a focused, healthy, and sound mind.

> Had He allowed His mind to be swayed by these distractions He would have never fulfilled His Kingdom assignment.

In this divine mindset, a problem becomes an opportunity to experience a miracle. A problem is God's way of showing you another dimension of His glorious power. When a problem arises, it's God's way of saying you haven't experienced my power in this way yet; you are getting ready to see God in a brand-new light. Many of us have the tendency to get frustrated and then we quit. We could be on the brink of a huge breakthrough, but we get frustrated because the process is taking too long, we quit and abort our miracle. As we embrace the mind of Christ we will have staying power because our focus is on what God is doing, not our circumstances. I heard Dr. LeRoy Thompson, a dear man of God, say that our circumstances are just the "circles we are standing in", they are not permanent. The mind of Christ enables us to change our circumstances and embrace or opportunities as we continually experience God's miracles.

THE POWER OF A THOUGHT

"Casting down arguments and every high thing that exalts itself against the knowledge of God, bringing every thought into captivity to the obedience of Christ." 2 Corinthians 10:5

We must remember that every word we speak starts with a thought. Once those words become prevailing thoughts in our minds they capture our attention. Whatever has your attention has your energy. Whatever has your energy, determines how you feel the next day and so forth. Have you ever wondered why there are days when you just feel "off" but cannot identify why? More than likely, something other than God's presence has captured your attention. What are you giving your energy to? What are you allowing to occupy room in your mind? God wants you to remove it. I believe God is saying it's time for you to be free of the things that have you captive; it's time to clear out the junk in your mind, much like you would clear out the old junk in your attic. Allow the Holy Spirit to discard what's no longer needed in your life and invite Him to refresh and upgrade your mind.

Fasting is an important tool for releasing spiritual cleansing in your life. Whenever I go on a fast, I begin by saying, "Lord I want to be closer to you." Many of us want God to sit on top of the junk that we have not moved out of our system. This is hindering us from moving in the purity of God. The goal is for us to begin to move into the deity of God. Jesus lived inside the deity of God, as a man. Even when His detractors tried to tempt or trick him, He stayed in the deity of God. They tried to get Him to walk in un-forgiveness but He stayed in deity of God. The sad thing is that many people of God fall away just because of one of these things. We know that un-forgiveness is a major culprit behind the lack of spiritual victory in many people's lives. Un-forgiveness holds a person captive; it holds you as a prisoner and you're the warden in your own self-imposed prison. You're the only one that can let yourself out. Unfortunately, many of us have made the choice to harbor every negative emotion and thought toward a person, instead of releasing it and allowing Christ to occupy that space.

Let me take this opportunity to describe the beauty of the mind of Christ. In 2 Timothy 1:7 it says, *"For God has not given us the spirit of fear but of power and love and of a sound mind."* The mind of Christ is a sound mind because the first thing He walks in is power. It's a common misconception that the Holy Spirit came just to give you the ability to speak in tongues. The Holy Spirit came to give you power - not just to prophesy or interpret dreams- but to deliver the power of God to you.

The first mechanism of power He gave to you is love. It's impossible to truly love people without the power of the Holy Spirit. With the mind of Christ, the first thing God is looking for you to do before you can walk in any miracle, is to walk in love. It is important to understand that your miracle will become tainted without love. For every healing and every miracle that Jesus did, it was done from the foundation of His undying love for His creation. Remember, no one in the New Testament was saved; yet Jesus healed every one of them that came to Him. That is love. We, on the other hand, refuse to deal with people because they are not saved. Some churches will not take up an offering to help you if you haven't paid tithes. A family may go to a church in need of help with a utility bill, and the first words uttered are, "Have they paid tithes?" We shouldn't allow a family's lights to be turned off because they haven't paid tithes. We have people in the church who pay tithes but are not faithful. If we do not walk in love we do not have a sound mind; we do not have the mind of Christ.

If you do not have the mind of Christ, then everything you do becomes what you've pre-determined, instead of what God requires. The mind of Christ can look past someone of a different color, of a different race, or of a different status and say we are one. We seem to forget that Abraham had all races inside of him and we have all come from his seed- the seed of Christ. When our mind is sound, everyone is treated the same way. We are at ease with everyone. The mind of Christ is only focused on the will of God. We should live in

If you do not have the mind of Christ, then everything you do becomes what you've pre-determined, instead of what God requires.

expectation of the manifestation of the sons of God. Note, I didn't say a Christian, but the manifest sons of God. Only a son can give the earth as an offering to God. God is raising a generation of sons of thunder who will have the mind of Christ, who will be focused on doing God's will. They will not care about money, status or anything else, only the will of the Father. The final revelation of Jesus Christ must return to the earth. Without the revelation of Jesus Christ, we are lost and our journey is meaningless.

PROPHETIC ACTIVATION PRAYER

The declaration of the mind of Christ:

- The mind of Christ is active in me today
- The mind of Christ governs me
- The mind of Christ governs my life
- The mind of Christ governs my dreams
- The mind of Christ governs my ministries
- The mind of Christ is strong in me
- The mind of Christ is sound in me
- The mind of Christ in me is the mind of love
- The mind of Christ is brilliant in me
- I possess the mind of Christ

I give Christ permission to govern and fully occupy my mind. I exchange my thoughts and images for His thoughts and images that I may be fully clothed with Christ's mind. According to 2 Corinthians 10:5 *(casting down arguments and every high thing that exalts itself against the knowledge of God, bringing every thought into captivity to the obedience of Christ)* Christ you are the one that gives life and power to this scripture. Therefore, I give you, Christ, the authority to destroy and bring to naught all previous thoughts, images, and memories which I have sown in my mind from past and sinful action and all illegal thoughts planted and sown by others that I gave permission to do so. Now, give me Your mind that is holy, pure and sanctified in Christ Jesus I pray. AMEN!

3

THE GOSPEL OF GOD

I WANT TO POINT out that there are three gospels; there is the Gospel of God, The Gospel of Christ and the Gospel of Nakedness:

- The Gospel of God is when God speaks directly to man from His mouth.

- The Gospel of Christ is when man takes what God said and performs it in the earth. It is the power of God displayed on the earth as man cooperates with the Spirit of Christ. Have you ever made the statement "I wonder what God will do next" or "I know there is more to God" or "I wonder what God is doing now?" These statements are all clues that you have been called to the Gospel of God!

- The Gospel of Nakedness is a false doctrine to reintroduce you to the power of sin and death. The agenda of the Gospel of Nakedness is to kill you.

Let's look at the word "origin." The definition of origin is "the place before reception." Matthew 4:4 says, *"But He answered and said, "It is written, 'Man shall not live by bread alone, but by every word that proceeds from the mouth of God.'"* Romans 1:1 states, *"Paul, a bondservant of Jesus Christ, called to be an apostle, separated to the gospel of God."* The first principle for those who receive this gospel is to separate and consecrate themselves to God. God will cause you to be separated from other people. This means that what Paul taught, he taught directly from the mouth of God! The Apostle Paul becomes the seed to this revelation and you and I will be the harvest that shall bring this back to earth; returning to the original gospel and placing man back in the original blessing of God.

GOD'S BIG PLAN

God's big plan is to return you to the original gospel: to move you from a lifestyle where there is a middleman (apart from Christ) between you and God. The first order of business is that there is a group of people in the Body of Christ that God will separate from being contaminated by the world. Some of you are already being separated; you just don't know it yet. You are being separated from

The Gospel of God is when God speaks
directly to man from His mouth.

your family, peers, the culture and from powerless religion because to move in this manner, God must bring you to the place where you are truly "one" with Him. The original man (Adam) ate the Word of God: all Adam did before he fell was eat from God's mouth. This is what God is trying to restore; He is trying to destroy all the confusion between Him and you.

> *"That I might be a minister of Jesus Christ to the Gentiles, ministering the gospel of God, that the offering of the Gentiles might be acceptable, sanctified by the Holy Spirit."* Romans 15:16

The original man (Adam) ate the Word of God.

The Gospel of God does two things:

1. Separates you to God, and
2. Makes you a servant of Jesus Christ. If you and I don't become servants of Jesus Christ we become dangerous agents of the Gospel of God.

Let's go look at a few scriptures:

- *"But even after we had suffered before and were spitefully treated at Philippi, as you know, we were bold in our God to speak to you the gospel of God in much conflict."* 1 Thessalonians 2:2

- *"For you remember, brethren, our labor and toil; for laboring night and day, that we might not be a burden to any*

of you, we preached to you the gospel of God." 1
Thessalonians 2:9

- *"For the time has come for judgment to begin at the house of God; and if it begins with us first, what will be the end of those who do not obey the gospel of God?"* 1 Peter 4:17

Unfortunately, the house of God (the church) has not been a good steward of the Word of God: we have diluted, polluted and altered it. People are pursuing things that were meant to pursue them. In many cases, the church has changed the purity of the Gospel of God and diluted the power of Christ. People are coming to church looking for someone to bless them when they should be the one releasing the blessing. You already have what you need but if you don't know that, you will always ask for what you already possess. Therefore, judgment begins in the house of God first.

God's big plan is to return you to the original gospel!

I was listening to a preacher and he shared a vision that God had given him. In a vision, God took him into the spiritual realm and He saw the Lord crying. He asked God Why He was crying. God showed him people doing things that were unclean. He asked God why he was showing him all of this and the Lord told him that it was because the church was doing the same thing. And the Lord continued weeping. I came to understand something the Bible declares in the book of Revelation, when it says, "And God will wipe away every tear from their eyes;" It can also be actually translated, and "And God will wipe away every tear from His eyes." This is because Jesus has been weeping since He left this planet because we have changed and altered what He brought to earth. We have more messages on wealth, money, and being a better you instead of messages on the Kingdom and the true Gospel! This wrong emphasis makes us change the purity of the Gospel. Material things are supposed to run after us if we first seek His Kingdom and His righteousness (Matthew 6:33). When you lose your way, it is always better to go back to the beginning and start again. We need to go back to our origins and God's original intent.

THE POWER OF REVELATION

The strength of this revelation (the revelation of Jesus Christ) will come upon you when you become a seeker (doer) not just a hearer. I want to give you scriptural references so when people ask you will already have the scriptures to back up your passion. It is true that faith cometh by hearing and hearing by the Word of God (Romans 10:17) but Jesus also said that it is when we seek that we will find (Luke 11:9). You must hear the Word and then seek or pursue its revelation. *"Have I committed an offence in abasing myself that ye might be exalted, because I have preached to you the gospel of God freely?"* 2 Corinthians 11:7

It is clear to me that when you start teaching the Gospel of God, you will offend some people. People don't want to be offended these days. We live in a world controlled and dominated by political correctness. As God and I began to talk more about this, He told me, we needed to be prepared, for the offense will accompany the revelation of the Gospel of God. Paul is an apostle who was born out of season. Peter and the other apostles walked with Jesus when He was on earth. Peter may have looked at Paul and said, I walked with the Lord, but how did you get all this revelation on Christ?" Maybe that is how they treated him, isn't this the way we usually treat people who we think are new comers? Sometimes we think that because we walked with someone for a long while that we are more special than the ones that just came in. I am convinced that some of people who will embrace and walk in the revelation of Jesus Christ, are not the people who are already in church today. God will use some veterans who have been in church for a long time who have also been waiting for this "Christ-like transformation," so that they can be changed into the image of God but it will be the newly saved that will come running into this revelation.

Paul was a murderer who was born out of season with whom no one wanted to fellowship. Some of the early Christians where even asking themselves if God had picked the right one. This man Paul, who was an outcast as far as the early church was concerned, was very intelligent but he was on the wrong road. He was being influenced by a wrong spirit when he was sovereignly handcuffed by the right spirit on his way to Damascus (Acts 9) and taught the Gospel of God. We later see Paul (a new comer) rebuking Peter (the veteran)!

Peter may have spent all those years with Jesus but he did not have the revelation of Jesus Christ as Paul did.

This is about to happen to many people in the Body of Christ: the Spirit of Christ is about to handcuff them and bring them in and the church is not going to have anything good to say about them. Because many of these people's backgrounds will be public knowledge and in many cases, they will have already been rejected by family members. But just as He did with Saul, when they learn the gospel from the mouth of God, they will be unstoppable.

LIVING FROM HIS MOUTH

"In whom the god of this world hath blinded the minds of them, which believe not, lest the light of the glorious gospel of Christ, who is the image of God, should shine unto them." 2 Corinthians 4:4

Let me show you the power of the Gospel of God. It's not just the words but it is also God's image revealed in us. When God returns you to His original gospel and you start talking to Him face-to-face He not only gives you the next-day word but he sends you away in His image. When you talk to him face-to-face, you enter into a face-to-face experience with God. When I say face-to-face I do not mean literally because no man can see God's face and live (Exodus 33:20); but I am referring to a more intimate relationship between you and God the Father. Adam and Eve didn't just fall from dominion: they also fell from a position of hearing and seeing God! Adam said "I hid myself because I heard your voice" (Gen 3:10). Adam had such an intimate relationship with the Father that they communicated thought-to-thought. Have you ever known someone so well that you knew what they were thinking? You could finish their sentences? That is the type of relationship the first son had with his Father. Unfortunately, he lost all that when he came into a fallen state; he lost that intimacy and now had to "hear" God with his physical ears. When that happened, Adam hid; that was probably the first time Adam heard God's audible voice and it frightened him. We know from the book of Psalm that God's voice sounds like thunder so that when Adam heard "thunder" for the first time, he hid. God doesn't want you to hear him only. He's longing for what was abandoned in the garden by a son. He wants you to see Him, feel Him, touch Him, smell Him; He wants all your senses to experience Him at the same time and not feel confused about what is taking place at that moment.

Everything that was created is alive; because it is alive it is aware of its surroundings. When God created the earth, the trees, the grass, the flowers, all of creation wanted a view of its creator. God formed a man from the dust of the ground and breathed into his nostrils the breath (spirit) of life and gave him his "IMAGE." Once Adam was created, it was his assignment to show the rest of creation what God looked like. Adam was literally God's face on earth

This is the Gospel of God: the exchange of
your life that others might see Him in you and choose
your God over other gods.

because he was the Gospel of God personified. Everything Adam knew is what God had told him. He embodied the Scripture, *"Man shall not live by bread alone but by every word that proceeds from the mouth of God"* (Matthew 4). We know that God met with Adam every day, Adam was the solution to all of creation because he was the image of God in the earth. When God created you, He was creating you to be the solution to a problem in the earth.

We must return to the Gospel of God. Phillip runs up to Jesus and says, "show us the Father;" to which Jesus replies, "When you see me, you've seen the Father!" In other words, Jesus was saying, "I am the answer to your curiosity!" We are living in the day and age where the whole world is waiting in travail for the manifestation of the sons of God (Romans 8:19)! The Gospel of God reveals to creation His face. When curiosity rises and creation longs to see its creator, God uses "you" to answer that curiosity. Let's go to the book of Job, which is the oldest book in the Bible. Before Moses started to write the first five books of the Bible, Job's encounter with God was already recorded. After his trials and suffering Job went to another level in God. Come with me to Job 42:5 *"I have heard of thee by the hearing of the ear: but now mine eye seeth thee."* Suffering is the catalyst God uses to separate you from the world and a religious spirit, so you can see God face-to-face. If Job, who is born of a woman, graduated from simply hearing God to seeing God, you can also graduate to that level of relationship!

THE POWER OF SONSHIP

God was trying to show us the power of "Sonship" through the life of Job. This is because only a true son will suffer for his Father and every Father will brag on his son when he graduates. Before Job graduated, God asked Satan, *"Have you considered my servant?"* (Job 1:8). It was Job that writes that he saw the sons of God gathering at the throne of God and the adversary was in their midst. Job saw the sons of God before they even came! You must understand that the things you are suffering now is preparing you for "Sonship." Every son must suffer in order to reign with Christ. Romans 8:18, *"For I reckon that the sufferings of this present time are not worthy to be compared with the glory which shall be revealed in us."* Well, ask yourself the question, "What's in you?" *CHRIST IN YOU IS THE HOPE OF GLORY!!* (Colossians 1:27) Which means the only way that glory comes out of you is through suffering! God is trying to kill the outward man so the ONE inside "YOU" can reign in life. Once what's in you is released onto your outward man you won't have to fight anymore!

You must be careful not to get mad or bitter in your suffering. Bitterness stops the Sonship process. Unforgiveness also stops this process! The hands of the very people He came to save killed Jesus. See, this is the call to the Gospel of God; understanding that you may be hurt by the very people you were called to help. Jesus says there no greater love than when a man lays down his life for a friend. This is the Gospel of God: the exchange of your life that others might see

Him in you and choose your God over other gods. Jesus puts it this way in Mathew 10:39, *"He that findeth his life shall lose it: and he that loseth his life for my sake shall find it."* He is not asking us to die physically but to die to self by responding in love even when our flesh wants to lash out. When you deny yourself, you reign with Jesus. When we came to Christ many of us were told that we could walk in the power of God but nobody told us that we first had to suffer for it. They told us we would reign in life with Jesus but didn't tell us how many times we would be betrayed, abused, taken advantage of, etc. Suffering is an event God allows to come in order to accomplish what teaching, prophesying or laying of hands can't do.

If you are suffering in order to reign with Christ, it also means that God is bragging on you in the spiritual realm to demonic principalities and powers!! He knows you are a true son who can withstand whatever the devil throws at you. God told me that He bragged on Job to the devil because He wanted to speed up his ascension into "Sonship." All the pain, the rejection and setbacks you may have gone through is because God chose to brag on you in front of your adversary. You must understand that God's ultimate agenda is to create sons! God is tired of us being spiritually immature. The only sure way for us to mature and become sons is through suffering.

SUFFERING TO REIGN

"Sonship" implies spiritual maturity. I always tell people that "offense" is a demonic spirit that God uses in your life to reveal your spiritual immaturity. Have you ever seen anyone who is offended?

They tell everyone within listening distance. Sometimes people will have a word for you from the Lord but will refuse to share it with you because they you are offended. The spirit of offense exposes what is in the heart. The Gospel of God is about God eliminating confusion, strife, and spiritual immaturity in the life of a child of God.

"For I reckon that the sufferings of this present time are not worthy to be compared with the glory, which shall be revealed in us" (Romans 8:18). Where is the glory of God? It's in you! But the only way for this glory to come out of you is through suffering! Job said, *'The thing I feared the most has come upon me!"* (Job 3:25). Job was living in fear. If you are living in fear you are not living in your assignment and full potential in Christ. Now, what I am attempting to demonstrate to you will not only show you how to walk in the glory but how you qualify for it. Some people will try to say that only Jesus can do those exploits but I want to prove differently. Job graduated from just hearing God to seeing God. We know he could hear God well because in Job 42:5 we learn, *"I have heard of thee by the hearing of the ear: but now mine eye seeth thee."* After Job suffered awhile he was restored to a greater glory. I believe this is what Adam had in the garden; not just hearing God but seeing him. What do I mean by seeing him? Everywhere Adam turned there was God. He was in the animals, He was in the trees, he was the water and the air; everything reflected God's character and His DNA.

In the fourth chapter of the book of Matthew, Jesus told the devil that it is written man shall not *"live by bread alone but by every word that proceeds from the mouth of God"* (Matthew 4:4). I know that Adam ate fruits and herbs but he also "ate" the Word that came out of God's mouth! Right now, the inhabitants of the earth are curious about the supernatural realm of God: that's why so many are dabbling in witchcraft and occult practices. God is going to bring us back to the Gospel of God! The first thing that is happening is you start sensing a separation from the world: even though you are around people, you feel out of place. You feel like something is calling you and you don't know what it is. It's the voice of God calling you into intimate relationship with Him, into Sonship.

THE SEEING GENERATION!

"I have heard of thee by the hearing of the ear: but now mine eye seeth thee." Job 42:5

When curiosity starts to rise in people about who the true God is, God will send you to demonstrate His presence to the curious heart. *"And the Lord spake unto Moses face to face, as a man speaketh unto his friend. And he turned again into the camp: but his servant Joshua, the son of Nun, a young man, departed not out of the tabernacle"* (Exodus 33:11). In the above scripture, we see Moses having a face-to-face encounter with God inside the tent, but another man was also there. Joshua was there and he was not planning on leaving. There is a second generation of God chasers that is just as hungry for God as the fathers are. This second generation is a generation of power demonstrators not just talkers. They are the seeing generation! Their miracles will cause people to ask, "Who is your God? How did you raise the dead?"

When Jesus was on the cross, His twelve disciples were there. They had heard about Jesus and they followed Him because they heard what Jesus taught. But on the Cross, Jesus encountered another group that said to Him, "If we see you get down from the cross, we will believe!" This means that Jesus ended a dispensation of hearing only and opened a dispensation of seeing! You are that generation that God has counted on to show his Glory!

The "heard" generation loved the anointing but the "seeing" generation is attracted to the glory! This generation loves to write books about the glory! They talk about the glory and pray about the glory. *This is the generation of them that seek him, that seek thy face, O Jacob. Selah"* (Psalms 24:6). What does seek mean in the above text? It means, "to go after without reservation!" When God says, "seek," He doesn't mean to just look because to look is an indication that you will stop if you can't find what you are looking for. On the other hand, to "seek" implies that you won't stop until you find what you are after! Seek means someone is calling me, pulling me, drawing me and I won't stop until I find him! This is why God says "Seek me with your whole heart!" When you find people, who are saying, "I won't go to sleep until I find Him!" he is part of that "seeing" generation that we are referring to! This generation includes those who are pregnant with the glory! Thank God for the anointing, but the anointing is God working with man; the Glory is God working all by Himself!

The "heard" generation loved the anointing but the "seeing" generation is attracted to the glory!

THE GOSPEL OF GOD

The Gospel of God is the image of God revealed in man!! The church was given the divine mandate to present "the Gospel of God" but for the most part, the Church has failed to walk in this assignment consistently. Spiritually speaking, the church is fat with endless sermons while the power of God is sadly lacking. Our desire to have nice things has polluted our pursuit for the things of God. I know that when my pursuit has become polluted, its proof I am looking but not seeking. Have you ever seen a woman who lost her earrings? She never stops searching until she finds her earrings. Seeking God must be carried with the same tenacity. This means that we must go beyond setbacks, pain, and sin and refuse to hear any other conversation if it does not line up with our desire to seek God.

The Body of Christ is reaching the point of no return! You are not going to go back to things that handcuffed and pulled you away from God! For some of you, the Lord kept you in church to keep you from the world but God was waiting for the right age and the right message to plug you into your destiny! God can hide you inside of the four-walls of the church even though most people don't even know who you are! You might be wondering why the leadership in the church has not called on you or promoted you. They are not supposed to because you have been set-aside for the Gospel of God! God will even hide you from you! Most of us try to be "seen and heard" before our God-appointed time.

✝

The Gospel of God is the image of
God revealed in man!

ARE YOU CARRYING YOUR OWN COFFIN?

Awhile back God said to me, "Son, are you aware that you are carrying your own coffin? As soon as you die to self, you will come alive to Christ and He will carry you." Many of us are trying to stand in the power of self at the exact time Christ is trying to stand in us! Christ is the Glory of the invisible God. Glory can only harmonize with Glory! This is why people who become one with the Gospel of God become uneasy with religious churches. Matthew 4:4 *"But He answered and said, "It is written, 'Man shall not live by bread alone, but by every word that proceeds from the mouth of God."* I want you to underline the word "alone" in this text. God wants to reintroduce you to the same place from which Adam fell!

When you are carrying the next-day move, you need someone to introduce you to it! When Mary and Elizabeth came together, the baby leaped in Elizabeth's womb (Luke 1)! There is a peculiar divine intimacy that the Gospel of God brings in the life of a believer. As stated earlier, this gospel eliminates the middleman. Every time a human agent speaks, some elements of the message from God gets smothered or altered before the word gets to you. The Gospel of God brings you past human agencies and causes you to feed directly from the mouth of God! The Gospel of God releases the power and image of God in the life of a child of God! The only reason many of us have "vain imaginations" is because we have not yet found our true image in Christ.

When Moses received the good report about the promised land, Joshua and Caleb delivered the report. Both men represent a generation. Caleb's name means bold and faithful. It takes these two anointings, boldness and faithfulness, to sustain the church. Joshua was the only one of the two who had access to the tent of meeting. Why? Joshua, whose name means "savior" had to receive the same grace that was upon Moses (his spiritual father). In the event of Moses' death Joshua needed the same spirit and grace that was upon Moses. This leads me to this statement; "the Joshua generation will not leave the "tent of meeting" until they get the same glory God has placed on the faces of the forefathers!"

This Joshua generation represents sons who bear the same glory, power, and authority of their father. They have proven to be faithful. They are chosen to walk in the glory that they witnessed their father walk in. They can be corrected without becoming offended; they are also warriors. This allows them to fight for their father while their father can receive the next-day word to release in the earth. The Joshua generation, are those that can echo and finish what their father started. They are a praying generation. This means that they pray before they act, not act then pray. They know when something has interrupted the move of God: they are not ashamed to throw themselves on the alter and wait for God to speak. They have the boldness to correct, without hesitation, what God revealed hinders the move of His glory. This generation can't be bought with fame, money, or titles. Their only interest is to bring the Glory out of the tent into the world. This gives you a better understanding why Caleb accompanied Joshua.

The Joshua generation pleases heaven so that heaven comes in agreement with what the Joshua generation is doing in the earth and releases the spirit of boldness and faith as Caleb's name represents. We have a glimpse of this in the book of Acts. As the apostles begin to move under the spirit of boldness Acts 4:31 says *"After they prayed the place where they were meeting was shaking and they were all filled with the Holy Spirit and spoke with word of God boldly."* As we move in the Gospel of God, we are accompanied with the spirit of boldness to accomplish in the earth what God is speaking from His mouth. Joshua represents a generation that was completely obedient to God; that is why he was so successful. He is that generation that heaven is longing to come in agreement to fulfill the Gospel of God. The Gospel of God is an invitation for mankind to return to his original blessing and in return, bring planet earth in alignment with what Jesus said in Matthew 6:10 *"Your Kingdom come, your will be done in earth as it is in heaven."*

All God ever wanted was a son, a family. This is a powerful statement, but this is the cry of the Father's heart, that he might speak to you face-to-face. The Gospel of God is a clarion call for the sons to return to the original order, where there is no man in between you and your Father. One of the signs of this gospel is that the preparation of the son is like the father. Note that in Joshua 5:15 Joshua is basically given the same invitation of his father. The commander of the Lord's Army replied, "Take of your sandals for the place where you are standing is holy and Josh did so." If you remember, the same angel gave the same charge to Joshua's spiritual father, Moses in Exodus 3:5. One of the things that the Gospel of God returns to the Body of Christ is the spirit of holiness. When Joshua removed his sandals, it signified that Joshua could now walk in the same blessing, dimension and authority of his father Moses. This is one of the failed blessings in the Body of Christ: sons cannot walk where their father has walked. This gospel returns this back to the Body of Christ releasing a powerful healing: fathers to sons, sons to the fathers, thus causing a major explosion in the Spirit of Christ.

One of the greatest blessings that the Gospel of God brings is the end of division. You and I can't be in Christ and remain divided. Christianity has been authorized to introduce you to the anointing but only Christ graduates you into the Glory. The problem with evolution is that it is designed to keep you away from the revelation of your creator. It is also designed to keep you away from the generational blessing that our forefathers Abraham, Isaac and Jacob experienced. Psalms 24:6 states *"This is the generation of them, that seek him, that*

Seek thy face, O Jacob Selah." What kind of generation is the writer talking about? This is the generation that flees division and seeks the face of its creator.

Let's study how Jacob received such a blessing. We know that Jacob's birth was unusual; when his mother was carrying him, there was a struggle or a battle in her womb. She was informed that she was carrying two nations in her womb. Genesis 25:23 *"And the Lord said to her, two nations are in thy womb and two manner of people shall be separated from thy bowels, and the one people shall be stronger than the other people and the elder shall serve the younger."* Before Jacob came into this world, he was already chosen. Ours is a chosen generation that shall rise in this gospel. Now let's watch the process of Jacob receiving this generational blessing. Genesis 27: 11, 15 *"And Jacob said to Rebekah his mother, "Look, Esau my brother is a hairy man, and I am a smooth-skinned man. Then Rebekah took the choice clothes of her elder son Esau, which were with her in the house, and put them on Jacob her younger son."* These two scriptures show us the revelation that Paul is trying to get across to us when he writes to the Roman church in Romans 13:14 NIV *"Rather clothe yourselves with the Lord Jesus Christ. So, Jacob and Esau show us a*

One of the greatest blessings that the Gospel of
God brings is the end of division.

mystery." What is even more profound is the process Jacob goes through to receive the blessing of his father. The mother is strategic in prepping him to receive the blessing. In Genesis 27, Jacob is explaining to his mother that his brother is extremely hairy. It's the mother who instructs him and prepares him to serve the father and then dresses him to receive the powerful generational blessing from his father. As I shared previously, it is critical that we submit to our spiritual mothers and fathers if we are to truly walk in our destiny. Jacob submitted to the wisdom of his mother and he received the blessing.

The Gospel of God returns the blessing back to the Body of Christ, in fact, it returns the original blessing we saw in the Garden of Eden when God said in Genesis 1:22 *"And God Blessed Them, Saying Be fruitful and multiply and fill the waters and the seas and let the birds multiply on the earth."* The Gospel of God not only returns fathers to sons and sons to fathers but also returns the mothers to the daughters and daughters to mothers. In this act, we see the importance of the mother: the blessing comes from the father but the preparation for the blessing comes from the mother. There is prophetic symbolism in this passage: Jacob puts on his elder brother's attire. Not only did he put on his elder brother's attire, with his mother's help, he also was bearing his aroma. We are to "put on Christ", our elder brother, and let the aroma of the crucified Jesus emanate from our being. As we put on the Lord Jesus Christ we graduate from our humanity to our divinity, and we can return to the Gospel of God, which is God speaking directly to you. Jacob shows us how we must do the same thing with Jesus Christ that Jacob did; dress like his elder brother to receive the blessing of his Father. Jesus is our elder brother and like Jacob we too must dress in our elder brother's attire and bath ourselves in His aroma. Put on the Lord Jesus Christ and make no provision for the flesh.

The blessing comes from the father but the preparation for the blessing comes from the mother.

THE GOSPEL OF CHRIST

I WOULD LIKE to introduce you to something called the Gospel of Christ. Many leaders in the church have set this ancient teaching aside because they have been pushing their own agendas. There are two things to remember: there is the Gospel of God and there is a Gospel of Christ. For about 21 days I was locked into God studying the Gospel of Christ. I was deeply engrossed in my study into the divine revelation of Christ when I realized this was my manifest destiny. I finally found what God had created me to do and be. I was created to bring the Gospel of Christ to the Body of Christ all over the world. After 15 years in the ministry, it feels so good to not have to prove why I should be in the ministry. Stepping into what God has called me to do has set me free on many levels.

So what is the Gospel of God and the Gospel of Christ?

- The Gospel of God is when God speaks to you from his mouth. Matthew 4:4 says that "man shall not live by bread alone." Every word that proceeds out of the mouth of God is the Gospel of God.

- The Gospel of Christ is the power of God in the earth.
  The Gospel of Christ is when man steps into his deity
  (divinity) and performs the will of God.

THE DICHOTOMY OF CHRIST

Isaiah 9:6 says, *"For unto us a child is born, unto us a son is given."* This verse is showing us two very important things. It is showing us that two prophetic actions are taking place at the same time. This Scripture has been the subject of theological scrutiny for many years. The prophet is prophesying that Jesus is the child born. Mary could not give birth to Christ since Christ is God's deity. He is God's Son. Jesus is the Son of man, whereas Christ is the Son of God. I want to make it clear; I am not dividing the two natures of the Messiah as though they are separate. However, what I do want to illustrate is the fact that without Christ, Jesus could not have accomplished anything.

Jesus represents the Lord's humanity, as such He wouldn't have walked on water without tapping into His divinity. He would not have multiplied fish, and he would not have been able to heal anyone. The Bible tells us that God is a Spirit (John 4:24) and because

The Gospel of Christ is when man steps into his deity
(divinity) and performs the will of God.

this is true, His only begotten Son must also be a Spirit. The "Son that is given" in the biblical text is Christ, the Spirit of God. The child that "is born" is Jesus. Jesus is Christ's humanity; Christ is Jesus' divinity. There is someone inside of you that is greater than your outward shell that everyone sees. The "One" inside of you is Christ and He is about to show Himself strong in your life. As I stated earlier, Jesus is the Son of man and Christ is the Son of God. Therefore, whenever you call yourself a son of God, it's because you have merged with Christ. You cannot be a son without Christ, living inside of you. This may sound brutal, but without Christ living inside of you, you are a bastard.

Jesus said unto him, *"The foxes have holes and the birds of the air have nests, but the son of man has no place to lay his head"* (Matthew 8:20). Jesus was describing himself in this passage. Ephesians 4:13 says, *"Until we all come to the unity of the faith and of knowledge of the son of God, to a perfect man, to the measure of the stature of the fullness of Christ."* You will notice that the biblical text here doesn't say the fullness of Jesus. Instead the Bible states that there will be people who will come into the fullness of Christ! If we just came into the full measure of Jesus, that by itself would be quite powerful because Jesus is Christ's humanity.

THE FULLNESS OF CHRIST

Ephesians 4:13 is suggesting that some people in the Body of Christ are getting ready to enter the fullness of God's deity! These people will be able to do things that have never been done before.

These people will be able to walk in supernatural power, which has never been seen or witnessed before. 2 John 1:9 says, *"Whosoever transgresses and abides not in the doctrine of Christ, has not God. He that abides in the doctrine of Christ, he has both the Father and the son."* It's fascinating that John uses the word transgress here because the word means "to rebel". As he teaches us in this text there is a doctrine called "CHRIST." Again, the Gospel of Christ is when man takes what God speaks from his mouth and performs it in the earth with the same spiritual authority and creativity as God himself. This scripture is not just providing instruction; it is a call to return to our original position that was held by Adam and Eve before the fall. Yes, this is a call for the Body of Christ to walk in full deity form in the earth; it must be taught as strenuously as we have taught other principles of the gospel. This scripture is calling for the Body of Christ to graduate from its teaching and preaching of Jesus only. Jesus is to be taught and preached to the unsaved the world and the deity of Christ must be taught to the Body of Christ. When we do that, we will see this greater revelation form a generation that will not be stopped or altered by anything this world offers them. If you are sensitive to the things of the Spirit I know you feel something greater is on the horizon; you can feel it, you can sense it, And I believe it is this teaching of the Gospel of Christ. We have not been exposed truly to our deity yet neither have we witnessed what I believe God the Father is yearning for His sons to govern planet earth and give him the greatest offering one can, an earth that looks like "HEAVEN."

BAPTIZED INTO CHRIST

"For as of you were baptized into Christ, you have put on Christ." In other words, it's saying there is a baptism of Christ coming to the rest of the Body of Christ around the world. Many of you have already experienced water baptism or have been baptized in the Holy Spirit, however, baptism into Christ is a different baptism. This is a baptism into the deity of God. A while back God blessed me with a vision showing me this baptism. I saw it come down and overtake several hundred people, and they were instantly changed! They sparkled like pure light. Their appearance was like nothing I have seen in this world. God is saying for those who have been baptized into Christ, (verse 28) *"there is neither Jew nor Greek, there is neither slave nor free, there is neither male nor female; for you are all one in Christ Jesus."* Galatians 3:27

Please take note that Paul, the apostle, did not say, "you were baptized into *Jesus.*" He said those who have been baptized into *Christ* have put on Christ. God is saying when He finds any "son" that has been submitted to Him, He is going to put back on them the glory that Adam lost. There are two Adams in the earth: the first Adam who is in a fallen state and the last Adam who became a life-giving spirit. You are in either the first Adam or you have stepped into the last Adam who is alive forevermore! Are you ready? God is about to put back on you the glory Adam had in the Garden of Eden.

Gospel of Christ is when man takes what God speaks from his mouth and performs it in the earth with the same spiritual authority and creativity as God himself.

You are about to do things that you have never done before in your life! You are about to step into supernatural power that cannot be controlled by human beings! You are about to become a "new creation" that has not been seen before!

Paul said "Christ in you" the hope of Glory (Colossians 1:27). There is a re-clothing God is about to do to His people. They will be clothed in Christ, the deity of God, and they will walk in power that has never been witnessed before. In the vision that God gave me, I saw rain coming down from heaven and it filled the house of God. The whole place was consumed with the spirit of Christ. The only reason why Jesus becomes the Son of God is because Jesus was in Christ. *"And no wonder! For Satan himself transforms himself into light."* 2 Corinthians 11:14

Transforming himself into an angel of light is how Lucifer can do what he does. Adam and Eve were living during an era when everything was totally innocent. Everything in the garden communicated so it wasn't abnormal for an animal to come up and talk to them, since they could communicate with everything. We must remember that most of us have only seen animals in their fallen state. A rattlesnake didn't possess venom until mankind fell. There was no reason to have poison inside the Garden of Eden. Consequently, there was no reason for Adam and Eve to doubt what they heard from the serpent. Thankfully, the Bible says, *"The earth is waiting for the manifestation of the Sons of God"* (Romans 8:19). The earth is waiting for the sons to get into their place so that creation can return to its original position. God has been waiting for His people to get into position, but we are too busy fighting about who doesn't like us in the church. If we're too busy looking at each other, we can't step into the deity of God. Too many times we feel as though what someone else has is what we should have: we have become extremely competitive. However, in Christ Jesus there is no room for competition for we are members of the same body.

AM I MY BROTHER'S KEEPER?

As previously stated, there is a baptism of Christ that is coming upon the Body of Christ. This is a spiritual dimension that has never been seen or witnessed before. As far as God is concerned He is still addressing a naked man. When you go to 2 John 1:9 it says, *"Whosoever transgresses abided not in the doctrine of Christ, has not God. He that abided in the doctrine of Christ has both the father and Son."* Adam was clearly functioning in the Gospel of Christ. When he fell, he lost Sonship not God. Almost immediately, he began to be ruled by the "Gospel of Nakedness." He is ruled by the Gospel of Nakedness, because nakedness leads to murder. This is how Cain got the idea to kill his bother.

Unfortunately, after man was kicked out of the garden, all he did was destroy whatever was in front of him. Consequently, when Jesus came, the whole world was spiritually naked. He had to re-clothe us, re-program us, and re-teach us that we are Sons. He chose twelve men and began to teach and show them their divine nature. One of the first lessons He taught them was to pray in this manner, "Our Father." He's not trying to be only God to you, He wants an intimate relationship between you and Him; He's trying to reintroduce you to your Father. God created everything you see and He's trying to share it with you as a son. When Jesus went to sleep in the back of a boat during a storm He didn't go to sleep because he was tired. He went to sleep, to test the men's deity. The disciples had been watching him for years, yet they still hadn't learned to function in Christ. The disciples wondered if He cared about them, and He wondered where was their faith! He arose and didn't address the wind or the storm. He simply stretched out his arms and said, "Peace be still." He did this because in "deity" you don't speak to the storm; you speak what is inside of you.

CHRIST IS HIGHER THAN APOSTLESHIP

The Bible says, *"The same one that descended is the same one that ascended"* (Ephesians 4:10-11). Christ was so powerful that you will never find any place in the Bible where Christ referred to himself as an apostle, a prophet, or a teacher. He never described himself using any of those terms (though men called Him that). Christ gave us the gifts of the apostles, prophets, evangelists, teachers, pastors, etc. (Ephesians 4:11). All of these five-fold ministry offices were inside of Him and He gave them to mankind. However, because

He did this because in "deity" you don't speak to the storm; you speak what is inside of you.

the power Christ moved in was more than most five-fold ministry officers could conceive, many of them reduced Him to a familiar term.

When you graduate into Christ, you don't need a title. Whatever is needed where I am, I can become. If a prophet is what is needed, it is what I become in Christ. If a healer is what is needed, it is what I become in Christ. In Christ, we should not be overly concerned with titles, because Christ is the hope of glory. Many of us have been taught wrong. This is why John the apostle emphasizes that we are to pursue love. Christ is love and once I step into love, I will not be prejudiced against whom I speak. Glory to God, there is a prophetic company of people who are about to come into the fullness of Christ. Jesus did not preach His own gospel. He said, *"The words I speak are those of my Father"* (John 12:49). He was carrying the Gospel of God with him. God wants you to be the one to do things that have never been done before. It's important to understand that the gospel of nakedness brings diseases like high blood pressure, cancers, etc. God wants to clothe you with a body that doesn't have diseases. The first Adam brought us the gospel of nakedness when he fell. Consequently, he opened the door for diseases, and all kinds of chaos. Therefore, we must, "put on the Lord Jesus Christ."

When you graduate into Christ, you don't need a title.

Lastly, Christ's seed is the mind of God. The Bible says, *"If any man be in Christ, he a new creature And behold all things become new"* (2 Cor 5:17). Adam originally possessed the mind of Christ because Adam did everything as if it was God in the earth. The mind of Christ is absent of any warfare, unhealthy thoughts, or vain imaginations. When Adam fell, he ceased to operate in such clarity; bringing total chaos to his mind and thoughts. As we saw in Chapter 2, mankind is always fighting a battle in their mind. The Gospel of Christ returns the mind of Christ to us causing us to function in the complete blessing of the Father.

God told me that as His people embrace this teaching they are in effect denouncing the Gospel of Nakedness. Under the Gospel of Nakedness many of us may feel as though something is missing in our lives. It doesn't matter how much we acquire and how good it feels in the process of acquiring it, we will be looking for more the very next day. We could have an enormous array of materials, accomplishments, and accolades in our possession and yet feel unsatisfied. Under the Gospel of Nakedness nothing is ever enough. However, the Bible tells us that in Christ we are complete (Col 2:10) This means that when you are in Christ your searching ceases.

We could have an enormous array of materials, accomplishments, and accolades in our possession and yet feel unsatisfied. Under the gospel of nakedness

THE GOSPEL OF NAKEDNESS

Because you say, 'I am rich, have become wealthy, and have need of nothing'—and do not know that you are wretched, miserable, poor, blind, and naked— I counsel you to buy from Me gold refined in the fire, that you may be rich; and white garments, that you may be clothed, that the shame of your nakedness may not be revealed; and anoint your eyes with eye salve, that you may see. Revelation 3:17-18

WHAT IS THE "Gospel of Nakedness"? This is a question that demands an immediate and honest answer. In this chapter, I will reveal an important and fundamental apostolic truth (doctrine) that has been hidden from many people in the Body of Christ. Many business leaders, including men and women who are called to preach the Gospel of Jesus Christ, have fallen prey to the devil for not understanding the "Gospel of Nakedness." Is this a new gospel I'm presenting to you? Absolutely not! This is my humble attempt, through the Spirit of God, to restore an apostolic truth that we have failed to teach the greater Body of Christ. The devil will no longer rob men and women of their future and God-given destiny using the far-reaching tentacles of the "Gospel of Nakedness."

Figure 1

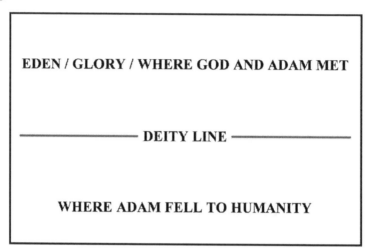

Figure 1 illustrates what happened in the fall of Adam and Eve. Adam and Eve were created to live and function in the Glory realm where God resides. In this realm, they were also clothed with the glory, therefore, they we never ashamed of their physical nakedness. As soon as they ate of the forbidden tree (the Tree of the Knowledge of Good and Evil, they were stripped naked of their God given dominion and glory. The above diagram also demonstrates what God had to do to restore us to our original position in Christ! The deity line represents a line God the Father was not going to cross to rescue mankind. Christ (the second member of the Godhead) had to cross the deity line and come as man to redeem us back to God as the God-man. For us to put on Christ and the glory we lost in the Garden of Eden, we must "put off" the Gospel of Nakedness that we received from Satan.

THERE IS A SNAKE IN MY GARDEN!

Let's look at Genesis 3:1-3, *"Now the serpent was more cunning than any beast of the field which the Lord God had made. And he said to the woman, "Has God indeed said, 'You shall not eat of every tree of the garden'?" And the woman said to the serpent, "We may eat the fruit of the trees of the garden; 3 but of the fruit of the tree which is in the midst of the garden, God has said, 'You shall not eat it, nor shall you touch it, lest you die.'"* I asked God, "Why did they (Adam and Eve) listen to the serpent?" The LORD said to me, "Son, you have to take into account a couple of things. Every animal in the Garden of Eden before the fall of man talked. Everything in the garden moved and lived on My Words, so why wouldn't they listen to it (the serpent)?" I was mesmerized by what the Holy Spirit was showing me. The LORD showed me that this serpent asked a question that the other animals didn't ask of Adam and Eve. This is where the Gospel of Nakedness was birthed, in the Garden of Eden. This is also why the last fight before Jesus was crucified, happened inside another garden, the Garden of Gethsemane. Jesus had to go back to a garden to destroy what was stripped from mankind in another garden over 6000 years earlier.

For us to put on Christ and the glory we lost
in the Garden of Eden, we must "put off
the gospel of nakedness.

"Then Jesus came with them to a place called Gethsemane, and said to the disciples, "Sit here while I go and pray over there." And He took with Him Peter and the two sons of Zebedee, and He began to be sorrowful and deeply distressed. Then He said to them, "My soul is exceedingly sorrowful, even to death. Stay here and watch with Me." He went a little farther and fell on His face, and prayed, saying, "O My Father, if it is possible, let this cup pass from Me; nevertheless, not as I will, but as You will." Matthew 26:36-39

From Genesis 3:1-11 there is a very interesting conversational thread that takes place between, Adam, Eve, the serpent and God. In the eleventh verse God said to Adam and Eve, *"Who told you that you were naked? Have you eaten from the tree of which I commanded you that you should not eat?"* Now everybody knows that the tree God was referencing is the 'tree of the knowledge of good and evil.' Everyone thinks that they (Adam and Eve) fell because they ate from the forbidden tree, but there is more to their fall than meets the eye. The essence of man's fall from dominion was more invasive than simply eating from the forbidden tree: having eaten from the forbidden tree, they became open and vulnerable to the preaching of another gospel.

Who have you allowed to pour another foreign teaching (gospel) in your spirit?"

WHO TOLD YOU? YOU ARE NAKED!

In the YLT version of the Bible, Genesis 3:11 reads, *"And He saith, 'Who hath declared to thee that thou [art] naked? Of the tree of which I have commanded thee not to eat, hast thou eaten?'"*

'Declare' in the above passage means, 'to make known, state clearly or to announce officially.' So in essence God asked them, "Who has declared to you or introduced you to a new teaching? Who have you allowed to pour another foreign teaching (gospel) in your spirit?" The LORD knew that from the time of their creation "they" (Adam and Eve) were under the Gospel of Christ but somebody had said something new to them. Please remember, whenever you declare something you are announcing officially what is about to happen to you. God told his servant Job, "you shall declare a thing and it shall be established unto you." What God is saying is simply this, "Whatever you and I declare, we are bringing it into existence!" When you make a declaration, you are making it clear that this is what is going to happen.

"And He said to them, I saw Satan fall like lightning from heaven," (Luke 10:18). In this powerful verse Jesus tells us that He saw Satan fall from heaven like lightning. But where did he (Satan) land? I believe that he fell into the Earth's atmosphere and then found his way into the Garden of Eden. When Satan took on the form of a serpent and talked to Adam and Eve they were in effect talking to a fallen angelic being who had fallen from Glory. He was stripped from his original glory and was clothed with good and evil instead. Lucifer's wisdom had become comingled with pure evil. He was having a conversation with them through the serpent's body but they

didn't know the conversation was actually a declaration. He was silently 'declaring' that they would soon be as 'naked' as he was. Adam and Eve were probably not aware that Lucifer, who was once heaven's light bearer, had been stripped of his glory and that he was now patrolling the earth as a fallen, naked being, spiritually speaking. He was alive but he was stripped naked of the glory he once enjoyed. God had already told Adam, "when you eat of the tree of the knowledge of good and evil you shall surely die!" However, when Adam ate of the forbidden tree he didn't die immediately, physically speaking, but he was immediately stripped naked of the glory of God that he once enjoyed! The Holy Spirit told me that, there is 'another gospel that strips men and women of the glory of God.' Most importantly much of this stripping is done through what may look like innocent conversation. You may be talking to people and you think it's just an innocent conversation, but while you are engaging in 'idle talk,' the agents of the Gospel of Nakedness are busy stripping you of your glory. Because of this stripping, before you know it, you will leave a place with people that love you. You may also discover that your business starts losing money or you start losing your emotional attachment to God himself. The primary

Everything in the garden moved and
lived on My Words, so why wouldn't they
listen to it (the serpent)?"

assignment of the demonic agents behind the Gospel of Nakedness, is to strip you of your anointing, your wealth, and whatever mantle or divine mandate you are carrying.

STOP IT!

Let me show you how to stop the Gospel of Nakedness right in its tracks. Satan is a 'glory stripped fallen angelic being' and as such he sows seed that causes men to fall from grace, while stripping them of the glory of their divine assignment. When Adam and Eve fell from grace they did so because they accepted the seed sown by the enemy of their soul. The demonic forces of darkness are all around us, attempting to use our desires to woo us away from our destiny through the unspoken conversation in our mind – remember, that is the battleground. Every seed produces after its own kind so because they are broke, they sow the seed and you hear yourself thinking "I'm broke." Because they are confused they sow the seed and you say, "I'm confused." Because they are in pain (or sick) they sow the thought, "I'm in pain, I'm sick." They sow seeds of death every time you say, "That tickled me to death or I'm dying to go." All the while you think it is innocent conversation when in reality those seeds that you've accepted are robbing you of your joy, stripping you of your glory, and causing you to forsake your destiny.

It is true that with the fall of Adam, God lost a son and Adam lost his glory but a tragedy that is often overlooked is that a new and strange gospel was planted on earth. One has only to look around to see what this strange gospel (called religion) has done to man;

whether it is a legalistic perspective of Christianity, the worship of false gods, the worship of man (secular humanism), or the total rejection of God (atheism), it is obvious that man has been stripped of the relationship he once had with God. Look at most nations today, they are void of true worship and are being hypnotized by false teachers who are teaching the masses that there are multiple ways to reach God or even worse yet, all "gods" are the same. These false prophets and counterfeit religions are stripping people of their desire to approach the living God and we now see men who are lovers of themselves (2 Timothy 3:2) and who call good bad and bad good. (Isaiah 5:20). God was showing that the same "Gospel of Nakedness" that is stripping nations of the glory of God is also stripping the church (Body of Christ) of its God given glory. Today's man-centric church says it wants to reach the children (youth) by letting them say and do anything. These kids come to the house of God dressed in ways that disrespect themselves and show no reverence for God. In many churches, they have kids and teenagers on the platform and pulpit under the guise of worshipping in dance when their dance is anything but worship! The pulpit used to be known as a holy, sacred ground: now compromise and corruption have crept into the church and some are now saying the pulpit is just the same as the seat in the back! The devil is a liar! The pulpit is the place where God speaks; it is holy and a place from where God makes His decrees. Unfortunately, we have turned the pulpit into a den of thieves.

God told me that we must overthrow these demonic agencies in the Body of Christ that are perpetuating the Gospel of Nakedness and stripping the bride of Christ of her glory. Today's powerless church doesn't cast out demons anymore. It simply talks about it. There isn't anything to talk about here; the devil has to go! The Gospel of Nakedness is a demonically engineered teaching that Satan presented to Adam and Eve. Consequently, we now have sickness and disease running rampant because of this catastrophic fall. The Gospel of Nakedness is designed not only to strip you of what you are carrying in the spirit, but the desired end-result is to kill you. You must become wise in your conversations! Avoid idle chatter particularly if it involves gossiping or slandering other born again believers, especially men of God. I'm going to show you how to cut off these idle conversations, quickly. The devil is truly cunning, but we are not ignorant of his devices. When Satan was speaking to Adam and Eve through the serpent's body he left enough truth in the conversation to keep them talking. Interestingly enough, all poison usually contains a life-giving substance mingled with something that is deadly.

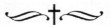

All the while you think it is innocent conversation
when in reality those seeds that you've accepted are
robbing you of your joy, stripping you of your glory,
and causing you to forsake your destiny.

"Now the serpent was more cunning than any beast of the field which the Lord God had made. And he said to the woman, "Has God indeed said, 'You shall not eat of every tree of the garden'?" And the woman said to the serpent, "We may eat the fruit of the trees of the garden; but of the fruit of the tree which is in the midst of the garden, God has said, 'You shall not eat it, nor shall you touch it, lest you die.'" Then the serpent said to the woman, "You will not surely die. For God knows that in the day you eat of it your eyes will be opened, and you will be like God, knowing good and evil." So when the woman saw that the tree was good for food, that it was pleasant to the eyes, and a tree desirable to make one wise, she took of its fruit and ate. She also gave to her husband with her, and he ate. Then the eyes of both of them were opened, and they knew that they were naked; and they sewed fig leaves together and made themselves coverings. And they heard the sound of the Lord God walking in the garden in the cool of the day, and Adam and his wife hid themselves from the presence of the Lord God among the trees of the garden. Then the Lord God called to Adam and said to him, "Where are you?" So he said, "I heard Your voice in the garden, and I was afraid because I was naked; and I hid myself." And He said, "Who told you that you were naked? Have you eaten from the tree of which I commanded you that you should not eat?" Genesis 3: 1-11

WATCH YOUR CONVERSATION!

Here is how to stop it: Philippians 1:27 declares, *"Only let your conversation be as it becometh the gospel of Christ."* All they (Adam and Eve) had to do was talk about the Gospel of Christ and the serpent would have left them in a hurry. Why? The answer is simple; the Gospel of Christ was what Adam was already walking in. All Adam had to do was remind the serpent what God had said.

However, he failed to do so and because he didn't respond with the Gospel of Christ, he left a door open for another kind of conversation.

Here is a real-life example to illustrate this important point. Let's take the case of a married woman who works with a single man. The single man walks up to her office cubicle because he senses that she may be having some marital problems. The single man seems concerned for her wellbeing and starts to soothe her. The woman, starved of emotional affection at home, suddenly opens up and tells him that she and her husband have been fighting at home. The first declaration the single man makes is in form of a question that is designed to make the woman question her husband's credibility and love for her. "How can a man fight with someone as beautiful as you?" He is declaring that she will not be with her husband for long. She responds by saying, "I will be okay, thank you for being so caring." She wipes her tears and gets out of this conversation. A week later, she goes back to work after another squabble with her husband, and by this time she is in the frame of mind that "I can't take this anymore!" She informs the single man who has been comforting and he responds, "You don't have to put up with this! Your husband just doesn't see that you are a good and beautiful woman. Why don't you move in with me for your peace of mind, until you figure out what you want to do next? I will sleep on the couch and let you have my bedroom." "Really, you would do that for me?" The woman responds incredulously. What the grieving woman does not know is that the seeds of an extramarital affair and divorce were sown when she entertained the first question. Satan is skilled in the art of camouflage and deception.

This is exactly what the serpent did to Adam and Eve. Lucifer, who was already stripped naked of his original glory, desired to do the same thing to Adam who was still clothed in the glory of God. Lucifer wanted what Adam had, dominion and kingship over planet earth. He thought he could recapture some of his lost glory if he placed man's glory on in exchange. Essentially, he was baiting them to trade in their glory for his nakedness. He knew that the woman (Eve) was emotional and he used her to start sowing seeds into a naked being. It wasn't long before they became just as naked and stripped of glory as the fallen angel they listened to. When I was writing this book, God told me that they are plenty agents of the Gospel of Nakedness in the world we live in. Some don't even know they are working under the influence of this demonic gospel. The Gospel of Nakedness is stripping the Church of her glory in the Lord. It's so tragic when believers sound like the world and dress like the world. When Jesus went into an unsaved house, the whole house got

When Jesus went into an unsaved house, the whole house got saved. He changed the spiritual climate of the people He encountered but they never changed who He was!

saved. He changed the spiritual climate of the people He encountered but they never changed who He was!

Some of you reading this book should have been doing greater things than what you are doing now! Chances are, an agent of the Gospel of Nakedness stopped you from walking in the good success the Lord ordained for you to enjoy. Just as you were about to walk into great success a demonic agent declared to you, "you are never going to leave the ranks of poverty!" Do you want to know when you are close to hitting your target? When people around you start falling off. Before you flow in what God has for you, He will start detaching you from toxic relationships. Before a rocket takes off into orbit parts of the rocket fall off! When things start falling off, you are about to liftoff into your higher calling in Christ Jesus. God showed me how we normally get emotionally attached to people who were never attached to us. They were actually agents of the Gospel of Nakedness in our lives but we never saw it because we were too emotionally involved with them. God told me that before we move into the fullness of the Christ Gospel, we must be stripped of the

They were actually agents of the gospel of nakedness in our lives but we never saw it because we were too emotionally involved with them.

Gospel of Nakedness. The Bible says that we are "to put on the Lord Jesus Christ!"

DON'T MESS WITH DELILAH!

Afterward it happened that he loved a woman in the Valley of Sorek, whose name was Delilah. And the lords of the Philistines came up to her and said to her, "Entice him, and find out where his great strength lies, and by what means we may overpower him, that we may bind him to afflict him; and every one of us will give you eleven hundred pieces of silver." So Delilah said to Samson, "Please tell me where your great strength lies, and with what you may be bound to afflict you." And Samson said to her, "If they bind me with seven fresh bowstrings, not yet dried, then I shall become weak, and be like any other man." Judges 16:4-7

The above passage from the book of Judges is one of the best examples of a true agent of the Gospel of Nakedness. Her name was Delilah, a beautiful and seductive Philistine woman! The only thing that I know of that assumes the status of perfection is true love. Lucifer is described in Ezekiel 18 as being perfect before he fell into the sin of pride; so, he must have been an angel of love! Consequently, the agents of the Gospel of Nakedness will target areas in your life where you feel you are missing love. This is where the conversations designed to strip you of your glory will focus.

Delilah was quite skillful at hiding her true motivation for sleeping with Samson. She was so good at hiding her real agenda that she got Samson to invite her back even after she showed that she intended to divulge the secret to his superhuman strength to her Philistine lords. She pressed him daily to reveal the secret behind his strength because she knew his weakness: he was looking for love in her lap. She was determined to use this weakness to strip him naked of the glory of his superhuman strength. Tired of being pressed for an answer every day, Samson made a foolish decision to tell her how he received his power. The Jezebel spirit also operates in much the same way as the Delilah spirit. She will entice you to let her in on your secrets, and then she will spring the trap – you are now in her vice-like grip. You become so ashamed at your foolishness and fearful that she will tell your secrets that you no longer fight against her. She has won!

DON'T PUT YOUR HEAD ON SATAN'S LAP!

Samson started to tell Delilah his heart's desires. God told me that the moment you release what He put in your heart, you have given permission to the agents of the Gospel of Nakedness to strip you of your glory because you have proven you don't deserve it. God also told me that the moment you share the problems you are having with your wife with another woman, you just slept with Delilah. You should never discuss your wife with another woman! Women, that goes for you too!

The more you fellowship with the agents of the Gospel of Nakedness, the more comfortable you become with compromise. Being comfortable with your enemies is not proof you are anointed. If you are comfortable, that means you are not chasing God. Passivity is proof you have settled and are saying to yourself "this is it!" But there is so much more that the Lord has for you! Passivity is the weapon that the agents of the Gospel of Nakedness will use to disarm you of your pursuit and God given assignment. The devil tried to use the Gospel of Nakedness on Jesus, when Satan said *"Cast yourself down, for it is written that the angels shall bear you up in their arms lest thy foot should durst against a stone"* (Matthew 4:6). However, the last Adam (Jesus) did not take Satan's bait, instead He quoted the Word! He declared, "Thou shall not tempt the Lord thy God!" Coincidentally, the first thing we must do when Satan is trying to strip us naked is declare what God has already declared over us! If somebody asks you if you are sick, please say, "NO, I am healed by the stripes of Jesus!" Don't agree with conversations that strip you of your glory!

The more you fellowship with the agents of the gospel of nakedness, the more comfortable you become with compromise.

PRAYER

Prayer of Activation:

"Heavenly Father, thank you for reintroducing me to myself. Before my mother and father conceived me, I was tucked away in the last Adam (Christ). But now I understand what's been robbing me of my success, of my peace, joy, and wealth. It is the Gospel of Nakedness. I denounce what Adam and Eve introduced into the garden that affected all of us. Heavenly Father I thank you for giving me the revelation that the last Adam (Christ) is a quickening spirit. I decree

and declare that everything that died in the first Adam has been made alive in the last Adam, who is the Lord Jesus Christ. I gladly allow him to deliver me from the Gospel of Nakedness that has been affecting me all my life, until now. I surrender to this divine stripping so that I may be clothed with Christ! Amen!"

CHRIST THE SEED

THERE ARE SO many things that can be said about a seed. For one, a seed is in the image of its creator. If the seed is the image of its creator, and if Christ is the seed, then you and I are the image of God. This chapter is designed to awaken a supernatural sense of awareness inside you that you are carrying a precious seed that will birth the image of your creator. Colossians 1:15 says, *"He is the image of the invisible God, the first born over of all creation."*

1. A seed is the image of its creator.

2. The seed holds the life of its creator.

3. A seed has hidden instructions, which are messages from its creator.

4. A seed has the power and authority of its creator.

5. A seed is the answer to earth's scarcity.

When God released you into this planet, He was responding to a need in the earth. That removes the thinking many of us create in our minds that we are useless. You are the answer to something that is lacking on earth. God came up with a solution for the earth before He answered your family's request for a baby. The Lord chose a family to bless when He sent you. That's why it grieves God when we make statements such as, "I would have been successful had I not been born into this family." When you make statements like this, you are insulting the power of a seed and the wisdom of the Creator. People say all the time "I could have made more out my life had I not come from this small town or this small city." God wants us to understand that for that city to function in fullness, that is where He had to send you.

CHANGE YOUR THINKING

First allow me to say, if you are going to follow Christ your mind must change. Change the way you see things and the way you perceive things. You must understand many of the things that are coming against you are designed by God and are part of His purpose for your life. The same spirit which confirmed Jesus' Sonship, is the same spirit that led Him in the wilderness to be tempted (Matthew 4). Likewise, God will allow you to be led into the wilderness whereby you have the opportunity to prove to Him that you are a son and are not attracted to temptation. If you are truly a son of God, you will not be engrossed in the things of the world and all the sin accompanying

A seed is in the image of its creator. A seed has the power and authority of its creator. A seed is the answer to earth's scarcity.

it. So, I say again, the first thing that must change is your mind. Our minds have been manipulated, programmed, and controlled by so many things we must de-program and then re-program them to align with the Word of God

There's so much being deposited into our minds daily, we can't possibly be aware of the impact of these subliminal messages. However, you find that as you attempt to accomplish your goals, all that input finds its way to the surface and impacts your decisions and actions. Many of us struggle to maneuver through life because of all the junk that is lodged into our minds. I say to you now, without Christ's help the negative stuff lodged in our minds will stay there. The strongholds of the mind are designed to prevent you from receiving what God has for you. This is why the Bible says, *"Let this mind be in you that was also in Christ Jesus"* (Philippians 2). His mind was not on things that He saw on this earth. When I make the statement that you are God's seed in answer to earth's lack, something should explode inside of you! I suggest to you if there is no explosion it is because you are still believing what has been previously said about you. If you are not convinced about who you are in Christ and are believing the foolishness spoken over you, you will fail to become the master of your own destiny.

THE POWER OF THE SPOKEN WORD

We must be careful of the words we receive if we are going to be successful in producing a healthy mind. It is often difficult for us to pull down these strongholds of the mind because we're looking for a quick fix. In our naivety, we think we can become like Christ overnight. But think about this, you didn't even become yourself overnight: it took time for us to create the messes we are in right now. This is a life journey that began the moment we were born. In some cases, our mothers didn't speak to us while we were in the womb, but others did. The negative words spoken over us penetrated our mother's womb and helped to shape us before we entered this world. Many of us came out fighting and cursing because no one undid that harmful damage; they just trusted we would be okay. It's hard to believe, but a lot of the turmoil we endure is because someone spoke words over us before we even entered this world. Spoken words are seeds. And every seed has the potential to produce a harvest.

Galatians 3:16 says, *"Now to Abraham and his seed were the promises made and not to seed as in many but as in ONE... And to THE SEED which is Christ."* God tucked that seed in Abraham to raise it to His glory, to control the earth. In the Garden of Eden, Eve took the fruit and gave it to her husband: however, the problem is not the fruit, it's the seed in the fruit. Everything starts with the seed, but our problem is we're too often chasing the fruit, instead of understanding the seed inside the fruit. Here is a principle, "when you kill a seed, you stop its fruit." Our issue is we love to chase things we can see; unaware that life is in the seed. Adam and Eve didn't know that when they bit into the forbidden fruit, they would also consume its seed. God raised a seed and wrapped a mystery around that seed, then tucked it inside of ordinary people. In Christ Jesus, God did all of this and the adversary didn't know that while he was chasing the fruit, God was moving the Christ-seed into position. God did just that; He tucked the Christ-seed in Abraham, Noah, Moses, David, and Aaron and so forth, until the fullness of times (Galatians 4). Our God is so brilliant and so amazing that He kept moving the Christ-seed so He could reach generations.

When he placed it in Noah we saw that the devourer that came to him was alcoholism. The devourer can seek out but it can't destroy what God has implanted in you. The prey can't destroy the seed; it can only cover it. Alcoholism got the best of Noah, but the prey could not destroy the seed. But remember, *"Greater is He that is in me, than he that is in the world"* (1John 4:4). Many people are busy looking for Christ and forgetting that His seed is alive in us and working mightily in us to make us Christ-like. The fruit is the least of your concerns; it is the seed that bears life. The seed bears the DNA of the fruit so what Adam and Eve really consumed was not so much the fruit but the information from that fruit, the DNA contained in the seed. Thus, a greater seed was needed to choke the seed swallowed by Adam and Eve and that greater seed is Christ.

The fruit is the least of your concerns;
it is the seed that bears life.

According to the book of Genesis, the tree they ate from was called the Tree of the Knowledge of Good and Evil. The knowledge Adam and Eve s wallowed was contained in a mixed seed of good and evil. The Bible says in Isaiah 45:7, *"I created the light and make the darkness. I send good times and bad times. I am the Lord who does all these things."* Without knowing it, Adam and Eve consumed a seed that was designed to replace God. After eating from the forbidden tree, they came into the knowledge of good and evil, just like God did. God is not trying to erase sin; He's trying to erase the seed that allows man to be his own judge of good and evil. God had to create a seed (Jesus) to kill the seed of the enemy (devourer) that we swallowed through our forefather, Adam. God wants to give you the ability to never be broken and lose your emotions to the evil one. There is a seed (Christ) inside of you that is greater than any emotional battle you face. There is a seed inside of you that is about to manifest. This Christ-seed will erase and eradicate everything that has ever been spoken over your life that is delaying you from walking into true Sonship! Christ is getting ready to rise and speak through you like never spoken before!

Pray this Prayer Out Loud!

I command the rains from heaven to water the seed inside of me called Christ that the harvest of his Divine nature may manifest right before my eyes. I give Christ permission to speak through me and work His works through me, in Christ Jesus I pray, Amen.

THE CHRIST GENERATION

1 Corinthians 1:7 says, *"So that you come short in no gift eagerly awaiting the revelation of our Lord Jesus Christ."* God the Father is eagerly waiting for you to get a revelation of the seed that

you are carrying which is the Lord Jesus Christ. One of the synonyms for revelation is the word "reveal." This mystery has been hidden from ages and generations past but is now being revealed through the apostles and prophets. This is the age of Christ. If this is the age of Christ, this must be the generation of Christ. There are three ways Christ was revealed: 1) Peter heard God say this is my beloved Son, 2) Paul had a face-to-face encounter with Christ, and 3) John the revelator was taken by an angel into the spirit and shown Christ. There are some people that are getting ready to press through the veil of humanity into the deity of God. It's time for you to believe that you are part of a prophetic company of people who are discovering the realities of the Christ within. Christ in you is the hope of glory and this hope of glory will overwhelm your flesh.

Let's revisit the story of Noah. God hid a seed inside Noah, which was the ark. Eight people went into the ark and keep in mind that the number eight means "new beginning." The ark is symbolic of Christ. Believe it or not, God is giving us a prophetic insight of the ark. The ark (was Christ) means that when we are in Christ we get a NEW beginning. Watch the power of this, while Noah and his family were in the ark, old things were washed away. When they finally came out of the Ark, all things around them were new. 2 Corinthians 5:17 says, *"If anyone is in Christ, he is a new creation. Old things have passed away and all things have become new."*

As we chronicle the Bible, we can see evidence of God stretching through the generations with His precious seed in the lives of Abraham and Moses. When God placed the seed in Abraham the enemy pursued it through Abraham's lies. Abraham's son does the same thing, so then a generational curse presents itself in this family. When God gets to Moses, He tucks the seed (Christ) in the Law, which becomes our schoolmaster leading us to Christ. The law is also symbolic of Christ and this can be concluded from His statement, *"Now I will write my law on your heart"* (Jeremiah 31:33). Moses' seed was uprooted by way of his anger and again the prey thinks it destroyed the seed. But the enemy still hasn't solved the mystery at this point. The devourer is hanging on to what God said (in the garden). Genesis 3:15 states, *"And I will put enmity between thee and the woman, and between thy seed and her seed; it shall bruise thy head, and thou shalt bruise his heel."* Here is the mystery, while Satan was looking for a man, God had created a seed. After Moses' anger gets the best of him, God releases the first priest which is Aaron.

Aaron, the first Levitical high priest was told to create a garment of beauty and glory. Which goes back *to "Christ in you, the hope of glory."* Therefore, the first garment was Christ! In between Exodus 28 and Numbers 20, we learn Miriam and Aaron insulted the leader. As a result, Aaron's seed was uprooted. He didn't know he released a toxin in the atmosphere called dishonor. I've heard my wife, Pastor April Roberson, a beloved and very knowledgeable woman of God say, "Dishonor is the quickest way to be replaced." That's a true and very powerful statement. Anytime you dishonor authority, God will replace you. And in this case, Miriam was stricken with leprosy, and had Aaron not had on the robe (Christ), he would have thus been replaced by way of death.

Although Miriam was stricken with this disease, nothing happened to Aaron because he had on the robe, which represents Christ! When you put on Christ no sickness or disease, can come against you because you are clothed in the armor of the Lord's glory. Numbers 20:28 says, *"And Moses stripped Aaron of his garments and put them on Aaron's son."* Notice Aaron is alive as long as he is wearing the priestly garments. I also want you to notice that no sickness attacked his body as long as he wore it. However, the moment Moses removed the priestly garment from Aaron, he fell and died. Before he died, Moses removed his priestly robes to dress another son. Jesus is our high priest and He has ascended into Heaven. He is now trying to clothe us in the same glory He walked in. He didn't need a garment in heaven. God took His garment (robes) on the cross to put on many sons that He's currently raising in the earth. This Christ mantle is going from son to son, and the whole earth is waiting and travailing for the manifestation of the sons of God (Romans 8:19).

Let's examine the scripture, Paul is giving us an indication that this has not yet occurred: this is an event that shortly shall come to pass. I believe we have entered the age of Christ and you and I are carrying a seed that is about to manifest in us. And the world is about to witness this manifestation. Remember, the strength of the seed is its creator and the power of the seed is its harvest. So, if Christ is the seed that is in us, can you imagine the harvest that is about to be witnessed in the earth? This has been carefully weighed by our Father who put this in motion before the world existed and had the adversary chasing shadows, not being aware of the power of the seed. When you understand what you are carrying you then become more protective of your surroundings and more selective of what you receive through preaching that does not lead to your manifestation as a son of God. I believe one of the main things that will trigger this event is there will be a return and hunger for order, not just any order but the Order of Melchezidek. Without this order, the sons cannot manifest. This then will lead the multitude of men and women back to a strong desire and passion for prayer.

When you stretch out your arms in prayer, the enemy releases an assault on you. But when we enter prayer, we also create a cloud of favor with God. He hides us in his glory so the adversary cannot see us. The adversary gets exhausted and gets confused and chases shadows looking for the Christ-seed in you. Spiritual darkness can only wear us down when we allow it to invade our space. Christ, the seed, is the mystery that Paul was talking about, and now this is the age of Christ. You are about to walk in the Christ spirit!

Prayer: Heavenly Father, I am aware there's a seed inside of me called Christ and you are the giver of that seed. I ask that you awaken the Christ, the Seed, in me and teach me how to merge with Christ so that we may be one in the earth; that He may govern me, my thoughts and even direct my actions that I may resemble Him in the earth. In Christ Jesus' name, Amen.

DESTROYING
THE BASTARD SEED

But if ye be without chastisement, whereof all are partakers, then are ye bastards, and not sons. Hebrews 12:8

THE WORD "bastard," according the Strong's Concordance (#3541) is defined as a person who is *"born, not in lawful wedlock, but of a concubine or female slave."* This definition of a bastard is very powerful and quite revealing. The above definition tells us that this person's birth was not legal; neither did this person's birth draw its strength, character and authority from the covenant called marriage.

Another equally important definition of a "bastard" is the one I received from my spiritual father, Dr. Francis Myles, "A bastard is a son without a divine pattern." There is a seed of the enemy that is actively working in most men and women, robbing them of their spiritual inheritance and God given destiny. This seed is called the bastard seed. This seed is designed to do one thing, to promote a person's gift, while their character never gets developed. A person who carries this bastard spirit will never accept the kind of necessary correction that is required for Christ to be fully formed in the life of a believer.

The bastard seed promotes one's gift and puts that gift on stage, so that the audience can be mesmerized by the gift. Unfortunately, the bastard seed does not allow one's character to be fully developed. Why? Because the purpose of the bastard spirit is to slowly and gradually move you away from the spiritual covering of your father. A person carrying the bastard seed will surround themselves with "yes" men and women who can never bring correction. On the other hand, your spiritual father is put in your life by God to help develop your character. Unfortunately, the bastard seed wars against the development of one's character, while the gift is being highlighted.

SUPPLANTING THE BASTARD SEED!

In this chapter, we will address the need and the importance of destroying the bastard seed that is operating in many men and women in the Body of Christ which has robbed them of having any real depth in Christ. Let's look at a story found in Luke 2:42-52. It is the story of Jesus when he was young. The Bible tells us that at the

The bastard seed promotes one's gift and puts that gift on stage, so that the audience can be mesmerized by the gift.

tender age of twelve years old, His parents found Him in the temple teaching. He was mesmerizing the priestly caste with his wisdom and understanding of the Torah. However, the problem with this story is that Jesus was missing for three days. His mother and father were desperately searching for him. No one knew where he was. His parents had assumed that Jesus was traveling with them. When they found out that he was missing they were quite alarmed, as any good parent would be. They went back to Jerusalem, searching for him everywhere. They finally found in Him in the temple.

This story is very powerful to me; I want you to see the prophetic implications of this story. When Mary went back to the temple in Jerusalem to retrieve her son, who was 12 years old at this stage, his response to her was *"How is it that ye sought me? Didn't you know that I must be about my Father's business?"* (Luke 2:29). Now listen to verse 51 *"And he went down with them, and came to Nazareth, and was subject unto them."* This is powerful; God showed me something explosive in this powerful revelation. The Holy Spirit showed me that at the age of 12, although Jesus was sent to save the world, His character was not fully developed yet. Additionally, the Lord showed me another important truth; He told me that "Many men

Bastard seed wars against the development of one's character being highlighted.

and women in the Body of Christ will have to go back to their original spiritual mother or father so their character can be fully developed." God wants their character to be fully developed so they can finish what God sent them to do on earth. I believe, we will see a revival of many men and women returning to their original spiritual mothers and fathers so their character can be developed. This is truly exciting and gives me tremendous hope for the Body of Christ.

I also want you to see something very powerful in Luke 2 verse 52. After Jesus left the temple in Jerusalem to go back home with his father and mother, I want you to take note of the fact that he submitted himself to his natural parents' authority. I am convinced the reason many people are not walking in what God has called them to do has to do with the issue of submission. Many people will only submit to the senior pastor (the set man of the church), but refuse to submit to his wife (the mother of the house) or the first lady of the church. My wife once told me, "it takes an Abraham and a Sarah to give birth to Isaac." I couldn't agree more! We will begin to see men and women who had left prematurely begin to return to their original spiritual fathers and mothers because they cannot go any further with their ministry until their character is fully developed.

I am convinced the reason many people are not walking in what God has called them to do has to do with the issue of submission.

Immediately after Jesus went home and submitted himself to his parents' parental authority it says, "And Jesus increased in wisdom and stature, and in favour with God and man!" This is powerful because it shows you what character does: character brings people into divine alignment and then releases favor with God and man.

IT STARTS WITH THE HEAVENLY FATHER!

Every son has a Heavenly Father who created him or her! Likewise, every son has a natural or spiritual father here on earth waiting to cultivate, equip and uncover what the Father in heaven sent the son to do here on earth. You just don't have a Spiritual Father that created you in heaven, you also have a spiritual father on earth to help develop your gift and godly character. Without following this pattern, the son will go astray. Paul said in 1 Corinthians 4:*15 "For though ye have ten thousand instructors in Christ, yet have ye not many fathers: for in Christ Jesus I have begotten you through the gospel."* Paul understood the power of a "father" in the Spirit. This is a powerful scripture that Paul the apostle is giving us. The problem that we have in the church today is the fact that we have access to too much information via the Internet. What do I mean by this? People have access to information that's on the Internet and many people who have a bastard seed then take this information into the house of God to challenge their spiritual fathers or mothers with it!

Your spiritual father and mother were not given to you by God so you can challenge them with information researched on

Google or gathered from social media platforms such as, Twitter YouTube and Facebook. God gave you a spiritual father or mother to help you develop your godly character. Most instructors cannot develop your character because they are too focused on celebrating your gift. A true spiritual father or mother positions you in such a way that the world will know you by your character: an instructor positions you so that the world will know you by your gift. A true spiritual father or mother is not threatened by one's gift because he is so focused on developing your character. An instructor is captivated by your gift; this blinds him or her to your character flaws. A father's correction is always pointed towards ones' character whereas many instructors' correction is pointed towards perfecting your gift. This attitude can lead a person that is being celebrated into arrogance, causing such a person to think that their gift is of more importance to God than their character.

THE VALUE OF DEVELOPING CHARACTER!

In keeping with the spirit of proper character development, at the tender age of twelve years old, Jesus returned home with his mother and father and submitted His life to them. We don't see Jesus again until after 18 years had passed. He reappears in the Gospels at the mature age of 30 years old. There are 18 years of character development between the time when Jesus was teaching in the temple and the time He was baptized in water for public ministry by the Prophet John. Please take note; something is spoken over Jesus at the age of 30 that was never spoken over his life when he was twelve years old. At the age of 30, after being baptized in water by John the Baptist, the heavens were opened over him as he came out of the water. God suddenly thundered these words, "This is my beloved Son in whom I am well pleased!" God did not say this when Jesus was twelve years old, when Mary and Joseph came to get him out of the temple. Why? It's because it took 18 years of submitting to his earthly parents to develop His godly character. Here is the million-dollar question, "If Jesus took 18 years to develop His godly character, how can we sidestep real character development?" We must also remember that Jesus never dealt with the "bastard seed" but all of us who are descendants of the first Adam are born with the "bastard seed" ingrained in the very fiber of our being. How can we hope to destroy this destructive seed of Satan, which is active in our lives, if we refuse to subject ourselves to God's process for character development? You and I must be willing to submit our gift, calling, and anointing at the feet of a God-given spiritual father or mother.

"If Jesus took 18 years to develop His godly character, how can we sidestep real character development?"

My friends, there are a lot of people operating in the Body of Christ that I would not hesitate to call bastards. Why do I say that? Because they cannot trace their lineage to a spiritual father or mother. If you cannot trace your spiritual lineage to a father in the faith, you are a bastard. When you read the Bible, most of the ancients didn't announce themselves by their individual names, instead they announced their father's name first. They would say, "I am the son of..." this is because lineage gives a person spiritual identity, depth and history. The absence of lineage means that you are parentless. In this chapter, I am attempting to destroy a demonic seed which is active in the Body of Christ. A true son will easily become the perfect offering for his father (e.g. Isaac or Jesus), whereas a bastard will expose his father's weakness (e.g. Ham, son of Noah). It's important to note that a bastard hates correction of any kind.

A true spiritual father or mother positions you in such a way that the world will know you by your character: an instructor positions you so that the world will know you by your gift.

INVESTIGATING THE BASTARD SPIRIT

Let's look at some of the characteristics of a bastard. A bastard

1) flees from authority
2) flees submission
3) despises correction
4) says, "I don't need a man's approval or affirmation to operate in the earth realm!"
5) says, "I don't need anyone's spiritual covering; Jesus is my covering!"

6) pursues fame and the spotlight

7) promotes their gift and introduce themselves by their gift

8) fails to acknowledge their spiritual father's importance and what the father has done to bring them to this point in their life.

9) loves competition more than cooperation

10) has trouble maintaining one spiritual place of development, even in the natural they usually hop from job to job. It's important for you to understand that your gift draws attention to you but your character draws attention to your divine assignment

To better understand the development of your character and better understand what God is trying to do with you, let's look at a very interesting chapter in Hebrews. Hebrews 12:5-6 *"My son, despise not thou the chastening of the Lord, nor faint when thou art rebuked of him: for whom the Lord loveth he chasteneth, and scourgeth every son whom he receiveth."* Paul, the apostle, is announcing two things that are happening in this text. Firstly, he declares, "whom the Lord loves, he chasteneth" and then "scourgeth every son whom He receives." Paul is showing us in the passage that 'correction' is for the one whom God loves. Secondly, a son also goes through a process called "scourging." Here is the million-dollar question, "If you can't get through correction, how can you go through the process of scourging, which is much tougher?"

Let us look at the word "scourge" closely; The best way to describe scourging is like this: Have you ever-made cookies before?

There is the dough and the cookie cutter. The dough represents you and your life; it is spread out all over the place. It has no shape or identity. The cookie cutter on the other hand represents Jesus. When God says He scourges every son He receives, He is literally saying He is taking Jesus Christ, the pattern son, and slamming Him against your life to get rid of the excess dough in your life. Everything in your life that does not measure up to God's pattern son is removed from your life. This is what the word "scourging" means as it is used in above passage of Scripture. Consequently, you can't come into true sonship without scourging. This is because scourging is reserved for true sons. When you enter this stage called "scourging," God begins to mold you for Himself and for His glory. Chastisement or correction is the first stage before entering true sonship. Every son will be challenged at some point in their spiritual development to prove if they are a bastard or a true son.

A true son is a revelation of the character of his father. While we are on the subject, "What is character?" Character is a set of values and convictions in a person's life that never change no matter what a person faces. A bastard on the other hand changes according to the mood of the crowd. A bastard's character is like that of a

Character is a set of values and convictions in a person's life that never change no matter what a person faces.

chameleon; it is constantly shifting to please people he or she is around or to enable him to gain the advantage. This is because bastards are driven by their gift with little or no thought given to their character. Consequently, a bastard loves competition, thrives on attention, and loves the spotlight. The biggest weakness of a bastard is in receiving correction; they take offense at someone "questioning" them in any way or suggesting that they are in error. Therefore, one of the stages of development that reveals the character of a bastard is the correction stage. Honestly speaking, none of us like correction but when a person fails to receive the Lord's correction they are a bastard.

THE HEART OF A BASTARD

There are two demonic spirits that drive the heart of a bastard. The first is a "vagabond spirit." By definition, a vagabond is someone who floats from place to place without having a home or a lineage. A vagabond is a person that cannot stay in one place. The second spirit that drives a bastard is a "jealous spirit." The jealousy inside the heart of a bastard drives them into competing with others instead of collaborating. A bastard is always in competition with someone even if the other party does not even know that they are competing against them. The spirit of jealousy is a spirit that screams, "Please look at me!" A true son's greatest desire is to become the perfect offering for his father. On the other hand, a bastard despises becoming an offering for his or her father because becoming an offering requires a person to lay down their life for another. This is something a bastard finds hard to do. To further understand this truth, we will visit the book of Genesis.

RE-DIGGING WELLS!

"And Isaac digged again the wells of water, which they had digged in the days of Abraham his father; for the Philistines had stopped them after the death of Abraham: and he called their names after the names by which his father had called them. And Isaac's servants digged in the valley, and found there a well of springing water. And the herdmen of Gerar did strive with Isaac's herdmen, saying, The water is ours: and he called the name of the well Esek; because they strove with him. And they digged another well, and strove for that also: and he called the name of it Sitnah. And he removed from thence, and digged another well; and for that they strove not: and he called the name of it Rehoboth; and he said, For now the Lord hath made room for us, and we shall be fruitful in the land. And he went up from thence to Beersheba. And the Lord appeared unto him the same night, and said, I am the God of Abraham thy father: fear not, for I am with thee, and will bless thee, and multiply thy seed for my servant Abraham's sake. And he builded an altar there, and called upon the name of the Lord, and pitched his tent there: and there Isaac's servants digged a well. Genesis 26: 18-25

This passage of scripture is very powerful. When you read this passage, it establishes Isaac as the son and Abraham as the father. What follows are the spiritual dynamics of a true father-son relationship that can advance the Kingdom of God. I observed two things in the above text that captured my attention.

1. The Philistines covered the water wells after Abraham died

2. Isaac started to re-dig the wells the Philistines had filled with dirt.

A son has permission to dig in his father's well but
does not have the authority to rename it.

When I saw these two factors God gave me a very powerful revelation. He said to me, "A son has permission to dig in his father's well but does not have the authority to rename it." The moment a son renames the father's well, he loses the authority and blessing of the well. Let's take a closer look at the sacred text. Who covered the well with dirt? The Philistines! The Philistines in this passage of Scripture represent the bastard seed. A Philistines is a person who is hostile, or of a different culture than ours, who has no understanding or appreciation of them. So in essence a Philistine is a bastard. A bastard will cover-up his father's accomplishments while a true son will praise and honor his father's accomplishments. It's important for us to take note that Isaac re-dug the well, he didn't rename it. This is because a true son's job is to make the father's well deeper, not to rename it. God used this passage to illustrate what was happening between my spiritual father, Dr. Francis Myles and me.

When I came up under the spiritual covering of this powerful man of God, I came into a revelation or a "well" called "Jump the Line." God showed Dr. Francis Myles how followers of Christ could break generational curses permanently through a powerful prophetic act that takes them through jumping over a red-line representing their corrupted ancestral bloodlines. This act of jumping the line releases them from the power of their corrupted ancestral bloodlines, into the incorruptible bloodline of Jesus. As soon as I started working with the man of God, God began to use me mightily to take this powerful teaching around the United States and Africa. As I began to share it around the United States, God began to give me fresh divine revelation as I labored in my spiritual father's "well."

TAKING YOUR INIQUITY TO COURT

The Lord gave me revelation on iniquity and how to take iniquity into the courtroom of heaven. The Lord also asked me if I knew why I was moving in such great authority and power. I humbly asked Him to tell me. "It is because you make your spiritual father's well deeper but you never tried to rename it." He declared. If I had been a bastard, I would have tried to change the name of the original well that God gave to my spiritual father after the Lord gave me the revelation on iniquity and on how to set up a court date to deal with iniquity in the heavenly courtroom. It would have no longer been called "Jump the Line." It would have been called something like "Line Jumpers" or variation of the original. Regrettably, the moment

A bastard will cover-up his father's accomplishments while a true son will praise and honor his father's accomplishments.

a spiritual son changes the name of the spiritual well that God gave to the spiritual father, the son loses the blessing and authority of that well. The Lord said to me, "only a father can name a well!"

There are three critical stages in the passage from Genesis 26 that every true son must prevail in. Please take note that every time Isaac re-dug one of his father's wells, someone came to oppose his forward advancement. The first place where he went to re-dig his father's well the herdsmen of Gerar came to him fight with him. They quarreled with him over the well, to such an extent that he moved away from the well which was named "Esek" meaning "to quarrel." Every true son must overcome the temptation to argue. There is no anointing in staying at the "place of argument." Bastards love to argue. When a bastard gets a glimpse of the forward movement of a true son, he or she sends out an invitation for that true son to enter a place of arguments. To a bastard, the argument is their reward, because bastards use these arguments to stop the movement of other spiritual sons and daughters.

I want to admonish every person who is reading this book not to get involved in unnecessary arguments or allow the spirit of strife to overtake you. It is worth noting that when an argument ensued, Isaac left the first well and moved to the next well his father Abraham had dug. He quickly and successfully re-dug this second well. This second well was known as "Sitnah". Immediately after Isaac re-dug the second well the Philistines once again fought with him over this well. Instead of staying to fight with them Isaac simply continued to move. Sitnah means "contention." I challenge every true son to cooperate with the Holy Spirit so you can overcome the spirit of contention. Every true son will come up against the spirit of opposition or contention. The Lord also showed me that contention is "controlled jealousy." In other words, contention is simmering jealousy under control for a fleeting moment. The spirit of contention will seriously challenge your sonship with unforeseen opposition from people you did not even realize where against you. True sons must know that it is not worth fighting over foolish things because they are secure in their true identity in Christ. If a true son doesn't get caught up in unnecessary arguments, quarreling or contention, he or she will be able to graduate to the third well, which is called "Rehoboth." "Rehoboth" means the "place of divine enlargement." The strategy of a bastard seed is to get you caught up in arguments, and all sorts of fights so you never make it to "Rehoboth," your place of enlargement. The danger of this seed being in the Body of Christ is that it not only robs us of our personal destiny and our assignments it stops us from developing into Fathers; thus, robbing future generations of this powerful blessing of God. Apostle Paul states in 1 Corinthians 4:15 *"For though ye have ten thousand instructors in Christ, yet have ye not many fathers: for in Christ Jesus I have begotten you through the gospel."* As you can see Apostle Paul had a strong cry for fathers. We must not allow this seed to rob the church of this much-needed blessing. I believe that the church is about to rise and destroy this seed so that the blessing of the father may be released in the Body of Christ thus releasing one of the greatest healings that the Body of Christ has ever seen. This is what Rehoboth represents, a place of enlargement, e.g., God expanding his heart as a Father with the church receiving this blessing and birthing it in the Body of Christ. It means fathers emerging that help developed us, enabling us to be fully equipped to walk in our identity; no longer warring in our minds, arguing, walking in contention or jealousy but living a life of true Sonship bringing honor to our spiritual fathers.

ABOUT THE AUTHOR

Lee C. Roberson serves as Apostle of Sons of God Embassy, Kingsland, Ga (USA). Apostle Lee C. Roberson has the Heart of the Father for the emerging generation. He impacts the lives of many through his prayers, prophetic insight and wisdom. He is known for his teaching and preaching of the word of God and has witnessed many signs and wonders in his ministry. He also moves in great revelation of the Spirit of God. He has been sent to raise up sons of God, to equip, and train them for their God-given assignment. He is truly fulfilling the call on his life by uncovering the gifts that lie within many. Apostle Roberson walks in wisdom beyond his years and with a humble heart he reaches many lost souls for the Kingdom of God. His first love is Evangelistic work but God has used him in various offices and giftings when needed to breathe life in and on those who have lost the very essence of life. God has anointed Apostle Roberson with the Holy Ghost and with Power and he goes about doing good, and healing all that are oppressed of the devil for truly God is with him. Apostle Roberson currently operates under the covering of his spiritual Father Apostle Francis Myles of Royal Priesthood Fellowship in Tempe, Az.